GCSE En...

Pride & Prejudice

by Jane Austen

Pride and Prejudice — it's five sisters, four weddings and no funerals. Unfortunately, that knowledge won't get you far in your GCSE essays.

Not to worry. This brilliant Text Guide explains the whole thing — characters, language, themes, historical background... the lot. And because it's a CGP book, we get straight to the point, with no needless rambling.

We've also included plenty of practice questions to test you on what you've learned, plus advice on how to plan and write top-grade answers in the exam! It's as desirable as Mr. Darcy after a dip in the pond.

The Text Guide

CONTENTS

Contents

Section Four — Themes

Section Five — Writer's Techniques

Section Six — Exam Advice

The Characters from 'Pride and Prejudice'
'Pride and Prejudice' Cartoon

Published by CGP

Editors:
Claire Boulter
Emma Crighton
Josephine Gibbons
Holly Poynton

Contributors:
Jane Bird
Holly Corfield-Carr
Marian Feeley
Murray Hamilton
Kate Redmond
Michael Southorn

With thanks to Jennifer Underwood and Elisabeth Sanderson for the proofreading.

Acknowledgements:
Cover Illustration by Juliana Giraud © 2011

Page 1: Fan Flirtation, 1908 by Glindoni, Henry Gillard (1852-1913) Private Collection/ © John Noott Galleries, Broadway, Worcestershire, UK/ The Bridgeman Art Library

Page 5: The Duchess of Richmond's Ball on the 15th June 1815 (oil on canvas) by Hillingford, Robert Alexander (1825-1904) The Trustees of the Goodwood Collection/ The Bridgeman Art Library

With thanks to BBC Photo Library for permission to use the images on pages 3, 36, 38, 39 & 42

With thanks to iStockphoto.com for permission to use the image on page 21

With thanks to Rex Features for permission to use the images on pages 3, 6, 16, 28, 43, 47, 48, 49 & 54

With thanks to The Moviestore Collection for permission to use the images on pages 3 & 25

With thanks to Alamy for permission to use the images on pages 3, 4, 5, 7, 9, 11, 12, 13, 14, 15, 17, 18, 19, 22, 24, 29, 30, 31, 32, 35, 37, 45, 46, 53, 56, 57 & 58

With thanks to Mary Evans Picture Library for permission to use the images on pages 1 & 2

With thanks to TopFoto for permission to use the images on pages 3, 4, 8 & 20 © TopFoto

Images on pages 3, 23, 33, 34 & 44 © WORKING TITLE / THE KOBAL COLLECTION

Images on pages 31 & 55 © WORKING TITLE / THE KOBAL COLLECTION / BAILEY, ALEX

ISBN: 978 1 84762 485 7
Printed by Elanders Ltd, Newcastle upon Tyne.
Clipart from Corel®

Based on the classic CGP style created by Richard Parsons.

Introducing 'Pride and Prejudice' and Austen

'Pride and Prejudice' is about love in Regency society

- *Pride and Prejudice* is Jane Austen's <u>most popular</u> novel, and one of the <u>best-loved</u> books in English literature.

- Although it's 200 years old, the novel's themes of <u>love</u>, <u>marriage</u> and <u>social class</u> are still relevant today. The basic plot has inspired many adaptations, including a <u>zombie</u> novel and a <u>Bollywood</u> musical.

Pride and Prejudice has two strong messages

1) People should marry for <u>love</u>, not <u>money</u> or <u>social status</u>. The characters who marry people they love are much <u>happier</u> than those who marry for other reasons.

2) <u>First impressions</u> are often <u>wrong</u> — it's a mistake to judge people on <u>shallow</u> qualities.

Jane Austen's writing was inspired by her own background

- Jane Austen's <u>background</u> is very <u>similar</u> to the background of her main characters. Her family were <u>minor gentry</u> (like the Bennets) who made their income <u>renting out</u> their land. Austen was also very close to her <u>sister</u> (like Elizabeth and Jane in the novel).

- She <u>never married</u>, although apparently she was in <u>love</u> once. She also <u>turned down</u> a proposal from another man, even though marrying him would have given her <u>financial security</u>.

- Although she had four books <u>published</u> in her lifetime, she never became <u>rich</u> and was <u>dependent</u> on her father or brothers for her entire life.

1775	Born in <u>Steventon</u> in Hampshire.
1795	Had a <u>romantic relationship</u> with Tom Lefroy, but didn't marry him — they were both too <u>poor</u>.
1802	Harris Bigg-Wither <u>proposed</u>. Austen <u>accepted</u> but <u>changed</u> her mind the next morning.
1805	Her father <u>died</u>. Austen was now dependent on her brothers.
1809	Moved to a <u>cottage</u> on her brother Edward's estate. Here Austen spent much of her time <u>writing</u>.
1811	'Sense and Sensibility' published.
1813	'<u>Pride and Prejudice</u>' published.
1814–15	'Mansfield Park' and 'Emma' published.
1817	<u>Died</u>, aged 41.

© Mary Evans / Retrograph Collection

Background Information

The novel is set in Hertfordshire, Kent and Derbyshire

Some of the places in the novel — such as towns like Brighton and counties like Hertfordshire — are <u>real</u>, but the town of Meryton and estates like Longbourn are <u>made up</u>. Here are the <u>key locations</u> in the novel:

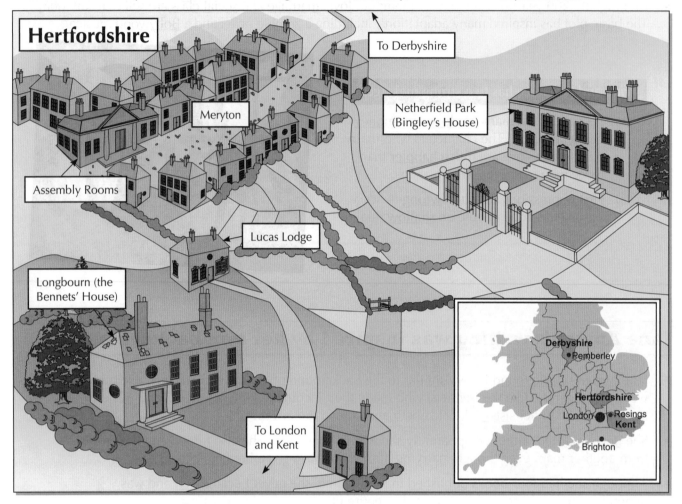

Hertfordshire

To Derbyshire

Meryton

Netherfield Park (Bingley's House)

Assembly Rooms

Lucas Lodge

Longbourn (the Bennets' House)

To London and Kent

Derbyshire
●Pemberley

Hertfordshire
London ●Rosings
Kent

Brighton

Women were expected to marry for financial security

© Mary Evans Picture Library

- During Jane Austen's time, it wasn't socially <u>acceptable</u> for <u>upper-class</u> women to <u>work</u>.

- If they didn't get married they usually had to <u>rely</u> on <u>family members</u> to support them.

- This put a lot of <u>pressure</u> on women to find a <u>rich</u> husband to <u>support</u> them.

- *Pride and Prejudice* explores the <u>problems</u> and <u>dilemmas</u> this creates for the Bennet sisters as they try to find happiness <u>and</u> financial security.

Introduction

Who's Who in 'Pride and Prejudice'

Elizabeth Bennet...

... is the heroine, and one of five sisters. She's got a good sense of humour, but she's quick to form opinions about people.

Mr Darcy...

... is a rich, handsome landowner with a high opinion of himself. He falls in love with Elizabeth.

Jane Bennet...

... is the eldest Bennet daughter. She's quiet and good-natured.

Mr Bingley...

... is a friend of Mr Darcy. He's rich, generous and easy-going.

Lydia Bennet...

... is the youngest Bennet daughter. She's flirty, and very keen on men in uniform.

George Wickham...

... is a handsome soldier with an eye for the ladies.

Mr and Mrs Bennet...

... are Elizabeth's parents. Mrs Bennet is silly and bad-mannered. Mr Bennet is sarcastic but he means well.

Charlotte Lucas...

... is Elizabeth's friend. She's practical and not romantic. She doesn't expect to marry for love.

Mr Collins...

... is the stupid heir to the Bennet estate. He looks down on the Bennets and worships Lady Catherine de Bourgh.

Lady Catherine de Bourgh...

... is Mr Darcy's rich, snobby aunt. She wants him to marry her daughter Anne.

'Pride and Prejudice' — Plot Summary

'Pride and Prejudice'... what happens when?

Here's a little recap of the main events of *Pride and Prejudice*. It's a good idea to learn what happens when, so that you know exactly how the plot progresses and how all the important events fit together.

Chapters 1 to 16 — The Bennets meet some single men

- A <u>young</u>, <u>single</u>, <u>rich</u> man called <u>Mr Bingley</u> rents a house near to the Bennets. Mrs Bennet hopes he'll marry one of her five daughters.

- There's a <u>ball</u> in Meryton — Bingley seems to like Jane Bennet, but his friend Darcy insults Elizabeth.

- A regiment of <u>soldiers</u> are stationed in the town.

- Jane becomes <u>ill</u> at Bingley's house and has to <u>stay</u> until she's better. Elizabeth goes to look after her.

- Darcy's <u>attracted</u> to Elizabeth but he doesn't like her <u>family</u>, so he tries to <u>ignore</u> her.

- <u>Mr Collins</u>, Mr Bennet's heir, comes to stay.

- A new officer arrives in town, called <u>Mr Wickham</u>. He tells Elizabeth that Darcy <u>cruelly</u> stopped him becoming a clergyman, leaving him with <u>no money</u>.

Chapters 17 to 26 — Elizabeth and Jane are disappointed in love

- Bingley has a <u>ball</u> and Elizabeth <u>asks</u> Darcy about his <u>behaviour</u> towards Wickham. He <u>changes</u> the subject.

- Mr Collins <u>proposes</u> to Elizabeth and she <u>refuses</u>.

- The Bingleys go to London.

- Mr Collins proposes to <u>Charlotte Lucas</u>, who <u>accepts</u>.

- Miss Bingley writes to Jane. She says that she expects Mr Bingley to <u>marry</u> Darcy's <u>sister</u>, and tells her they won't <u>come back</u> to Meryton.

- Jane goes to <u>London</u> with her aunt and uncle. She <u>visits</u> Miss Bingley, who treats her <u>rudely</u>.

- Wickham stops flirting with Elizabeth and pays more attention to a girl who's inherited lots of <u>money</u>.

Introduction

Chapters 27 to 45 — Elizabeth and Darcy change their opinions

- Elizabeth <u>visits</u> Charlotte and Mr Collins in Kent. They go to <u>Lady Catherine de Bourgh's</u> for dinner.

- <u>Darcy</u> visits Lady Catherine and sees <u>Elizabeth</u> quite frequently.

- Elizabeth finds out from Colonel Fitzwilliam that <u>Darcy</u> told Bingley not to <u>marry Jane</u>. She assumes it was because of her <u>family</u>.

- Darcy <u>proposes</u> to Elizabeth. She <u>refuses</u>, and accuses him of treating Wickham <u>unfairly</u> and <u>ruining</u> Jane's hopes of happiness.

© AF archive / Alamy

- Darcy writes Elizabeth a <u>letter</u> explaining that he didn't think Jane <u>loved</u> Bingley. He also tells her that Wickham tried to <u>elope</u> with Darcy's fifteen year-old sister to get her <u>fortune</u>.

- The regiment of <u>soldiers</u> moves to Brighton and <u>Lydia</u> is <u>invited</u> to stay with one of the officer's wives.

- Elizabeth goes on <u>holiday</u> with the Gardiners. They visit Darcy's <u>stately home</u> in Derbyshire, and bump into Darcy, who is <u>friendly</u> and <u>charming</u>.

Chapters 46 to 61 — Three weddings and a scandal

- Elizabeth finds out that Lydia has <u>run away</u> with Wickham, and goes home at once.

- <u>Mr Gardiner</u> tells the Bennets that Lydia and Wickham have been <u>found</u>, and that Wickham has agreed to <u>marry Lydia</u>.

© AF archive / Alamy

- Elizabeth learns it was <u>Darcy</u> who saved the family from disgrace by <u>bribing</u> Wickham to <u>marry</u> Lydia.

- Bingley returns from London, and <u>proposes</u> to Jane.

- Lady Catherine <u>visits</u> Elizabeth because she's heard that Elizabeth and Darcy are <u>engaged</u>. She tells Elizabeth that she must promise <u>not</u> to marry him, but Elizabeth <u>refuses</u>.

- Darcy visits, and <u>proposes</u> to Elizabeth <u>again</u>. This time she <u>accepts</u>. Everyone lives <u>happily ever after</u>.

Lizzy and Darcy, sitting in a tree, K-I-S-S-I-N-G...

...but only after they've been legally joined in holy matrimony, obviously. Once you're confident you know what happens in *Pride and Prejudice*, you're ready to start Section One. If you're still unsure about the novel's plot or want a break from revision, have a look at the cartoon at the back of the book.

Section One — Background and Context

What Life Was Like in Regency Britain

Pride and Prejudice was written about 200 years ago, and things were pretty different back then.

'Pride and Prejudice' was first published in 1813

1) *Pride and Prejudice* was <u>first published</u> in <u>1813</u>, in the <u>Regency Period</u> (named after the <u>Prince Regent</u>).

> *A Prince Regent is a prince who rules a country while the king is still alive, because the king isn't capable of it.*

2) The Regency Period came after the <u>Georgian era</u> and just before the <u>Victorian era</u>.

3) England was <u>at war</u> with France, which explains the <u>regiments of soldiers</u> stationed all over the south of England in the novel.

4) Society was very <u>stratified</u> — different social groups <u>didn't mix much</u> and there was a <u>big gap</u> between the <u>rich</u> and the <u>poor</u>.

> Austen <u>doesn't</u> write much about the very lowest or highest levels of society — she focuses on the <u>upper middle classes</u>. This is the class Austen belonged to, so she's writing about what she <u>knows</u>.

England was a rural society

1) England was a <u>rural society</u> during the Regency Period — most people lived in the <u>countryside</u> (nowadays most people live in towns or cities).

2) Lots of characters in the novel <u>own farmland</u>, e.g.

- <u>Darcy</u> owns a "<u>large</u> estate in Derbyshire". He doesn't run the farms on it <u>himself</u>, but lives off the profits from <u>renting</u> it out.

- <u>Mr Bennet</u> owns an estate (much smaller than Darcy's), which includes <u>farmland</u>.

© Everett Collection/Rex Features

England was on the verge of big changes

1) *Pride and Prejudice* was written during the <u>Industrial Revolution</u>.

2) <u>Before</u> the Industrial Revolution, society was <u>divided</u> between the <u>very rich</u> upper classes and the <u>poor working classes</u>. Land and money were controlled by a <u>few</u> rich powerful <u>families</u> and passed down through <u>inheritance</u>, so there was little chance for people from <u>lower</u> social classes to become <u>wealthy</u>.

3) <u>During</u> the Industrial Revolution, machines for <u>manufacturing</u> and <u>transport</u> improved — this meant that <u>businesses</u> could make and trade their products <u>quickly</u> and <u>cheaply</u>.

4) This made it possible for working-class people to <u>earn</u> more money instead of <u>inheriting</u> it, so there wasn't such a <u>big divide</u> of wealth. Some people from <u>lower</u> social classes became quite <u>well-off</u>.

5) A <u>few</u> people became <u>really rich</u>, which meant they could start <u>mixing</u> with the upper classes.

> **Theme — Social Class**
>
> Austen doesn't write about these changes <u>directly</u>, but the <u>snobbish attitudes</u> of characters like Lady Catherine show how wealthy people from "ancient families" felt <u>threatened</u> by those with '<u>new money</u>'. The <u>Bingleys</u> are rich through "trade" — Miss Bingley is sensitive about this, so she <u>criticises others</u>.

What Life Was Like in Regency Britain

The holidays in the novel might seem dull now — travel was tricky, so a weekend in Ibiza was definitely out.

It wasn't easy to get around

1) In the Regency Period journeys were on <u>horseback</u>, by <u>horse and carriage</u>, or simply on <u>foot</u>.

2) <u>Gentlewomen</u> usually rode in a <u>carriage</u>, as this was considered the more <u>ladylike</u> thing to do. Carriages were <u>slow</u>, so travel was limited. However, it was <u>acceptable</u> for a <u>man</u> to travel alone on horseback.

3) Travel was <u>expensive</u> — only quite rich people could afford a horse and carriage.

4) Darcy and Elizabeth view travel <u>differently</u> — e.g. when they talk about Charlotte moving to Kent:

> Elizabeth: "An easy distance do you call it? It is nearly <u>fifty miles</u>."
> Darcy: "And what is fifty miles of good road? Little more than half a day's journey. Yes, I call it a *very* easy distance."

Darcy doesn't think about the cost of the journey, only the time it would take. His ability to travel is less restricted because he's rich and a man.

Holidays had to be quite local

1) <u>Foreign</u> travel <u>wasn't</u> really possible for most people, so English people tended to take holidays in England.

2) Elizabeth is <u>very excited</u> at the idea of going to the <u>Lake District</u> with her aunt and uncle, but even this <u>isn't possible</u> when their trip has to be cut back to 'only' three weeks.

3) Tourists enjoyed looking around <u>stately homes</u> — this sounds like a <u>modern</u> idea, but actually it first became popular in the <u>eighteenth century</u>. Elizabeth and her relatives visit <u>Pemberley</u> as tourists.

Socialising was very formal

1) There were <u>strict rules</u> about socialising in Austen's day. You had to be <u>formally introduced</u> before you could speak to someone. <u>Mr Collins</u> embarrassingly ignores this rule in Chapter 18.

2) <u>Social calls</u> to new people had to be done in a certain way — e.g. the Bennet women can't meet Mr Bingley until Mr Bennet has been to visit him.

3) Socialising happened at <u>people's houses</u> or at local <u>public gatherings</u> like balls. These public assemblies, where key characters meet and interact, are <u>very important events</u> in the novel.

© AF archive / Alamy

Theme — Marriage
<u>Balls</u> and assemblies were often the <u>only</u> opportunity for women to <u>socialise</u> with new people and meet potential <u>husbands</u>.

KEY QUOTE *"nobody can ever be introduced in a ball-room."*
Elizabeth is being <u>ironic</u> here (see p.55) — balls were a very common way of meeting new people in the Regency period. But you had to do it right — social rules were strict and complicated back then.

Women in Regency Society

Women were often treated like second-class citizens — they didn't have the same rights as men.

Property was often entailed away from women

1) Property was often <u>entailed</u>, which meant there were <u>legal rules</u> about who could <u>inherit</u> it. Usually the <u>eldest son</u> would inherit the house and land. This kept the estate <u>whole</u>, rather than <u>splitting it</u> between lots of children when their father died.

2) Legal rules often meant women couldn't inherit the <u>estate</u>. If there were no sons, it passed to the <u>nearest</u> male relative.

3) <u>Mr Bennet's estate</u> is entailed, meaning it'll pass to <u>Mr Collins</u>, a distant cousin, when Mr Bennet dies.

> **Writer's Techniques — Plot**
>
> The <u>entailment</u> is important to the <u>plot</u> of the novel. It makes the <u>financial future</u> of the Bennet sisters very <u>uncertain</u>, so it's almost <u>essential</u> that one of them marries a <u>rich</u> man.

Marrying a rich man gave women financial security

1) Upper- and middle-class women couldn't usually <u>earn money</u>. Some couldn't <u>inherit</u> either.

2) Their best chance of a <u>stable financial future</u> was a good <u>marriage</u>. This is why Mrs Bennet is so <u>desperate</u> for her daughters to find good husbands.

3) Many women didn't have any <u>financial assets</u> to attract a husband, so it was important for them to be <u>pretty</u> and have a good <u>reputation</u>.

4) Women often weren't properly <u>educated</u> — it was seen as unnecessary, as they weren't expected to have a job or be involved in politics or the running of estates. Instead they learnt <u>skills</u> that would <u>attract</u> a <u>husband</u>, such as singing or dancing.

© TopFoto

Austen celebrates women with independent spirits

1) It was almost <u>impossible</u> for women at that time to be independent of men. They couldn't vote and had <u>few rights</u>. But Austen <u>valued</u> women with <u>independent spirits</u>, like Elizabeth.

2) It's Elizabeth's "<u>liveliness of... mind</u>" that <u>attracts Darcy</u>. She points out "I roused, and interested you, because I was so unlike" other women (like Miss Bingley), who only act to please and impress Darcy.

3) She's <u>rewarded</u> with a relationship that seems as <u>equal</u> as was possible then, and Georgiana learns about marriage from Elizabeth and "began to comprehend that a woman may take <u>liberties</u> with her husband".

> **Theme — Love**
>
> Austen is showing that <u>personality</u> is more important than <u>social class</u> when it comes to <u>love</u>.

Mention the variety of strong-willed women...

EXAM TIP

You can impress the examiner by pointing out that Elizabeth's not the only headstrong woman in the novel. Women like Mrs Bennet and Lady C might not always be likeable, but they certainly speak their minds...

Jobs in Regency Society

This was a time when people looked down on you if you did more than sit on your backside all day. Weird.

The upper classes looked down on professionals

1) The <u>highest</u> level of the upper classes was the <u>aristocracy</u> (e.g. Lady Catherine). The <u>next</u> level down was the <u>gentry</u> (e.g. Darcy, the Bennets) and <u>below</u> them were the <u>professional middle classes</u>.

2) People in the <u>upper classes</u> didn't need to work because they earned money from their <u>land</u>.

3) Their money came from the <u>rent</u> they charged their <u>tenants</u> (the ordinary people who lived on the estates). The amount of money they made depended on how much land they owned — so Mr Darcy is much richer than <u>Mr Bennet</u>, because his estate is much <u>bigger</u>.

4) People who earned money from a <u>profession</u> or from <u>trade</u> (owning their own business, as the Gardiners do) were often <u>looked down on</u> by people who didn't need to work.

There are three main professions in the novel

1) Some characters are part of the <u>clergy</u> — this means they work for the <u>church</u>, e.g. Mr Collins.

- Being a clergyman could be a <u>comfortable</u> and <u>well-paid</u> job. Mr Collins got "early and unexpected <u>prosperity</u>" from Lady Catherine's offer of a job as vicar on her estate.
- It was often up to a <u>rich landowner</u> (such as Lady Catherine), to choose the local vicar of a parish.
- Being a clergyman has given Mr Collins a <u>decent rank</u> in society — he socialises with <u>aristocrats</u>.

2) Other characters are in the <u>military</u>, like <u>Wickham</u> or <u>Colonel Fitzwilliam</u>.

- During much of Austen's life, England was <u>at war</u> with <u>France</u>, and <u>soldiers</u> appear a lot in the novel.
- Wickham is in the <u>militia</u>. The militia protected England from <u>invasion</u> and stopped <u>riots</u>.
- Colonel Fitzwilliam is a '<u>regular</u>' soldier. They were <u>career soldiers</u> and sometimes <u>fought overseas</u>. They had a higher status than the militia — you needed <u>money</u> to be an officer in the regulars.

3) The Bennets have some <u>connections</u> with people who work as <u>lawyers</u>:

- Elizabeth's uncle, Mr Philips, is a <u>lawyer</u>. So was her grandfather (Mrs Bennet's father).
- The more snobbish characters <u>look down</u> on Elizabeth because of this connection. E.g. Mrs Hurst and Miss Bingley "both <u>laughed</u> heartily" when they discussed her uncles' jobs, even though their own fortune was "acquired by trade".

Comment on the effect relatives had on reputation...

Unfortunately, the fact that the Bennets have relatives who actually *work* for a living is enough to make the gentry look down on them, even though the law was considered a respectable profession at the time.

Practice Questions

Lucky you — a whole page of practice questions to make sure you've taken in everything in this section. The quick questions should ease you in — you just need to write a few words for each. The in-depth ones require a bit more effort, but a paragraph or so of your finest thoughts and insights should do the trick. Piece of cake...

Quick Questions

1) What is the name of the period that *Pride and Prejudice* is set in?

2) Give two examples of the strict rules about socialising that appear in *Pride and Prejudice*.

3) In *Pride and Prejudice* Mr Bennet's estate is entailed. What does this mean?

4) Which of the following statements about women in Austen's time is NOT true?
   a) They couldn't inherit money.
   b) It was considered unfeminine for women to be as educated as men.
   c) They couldn't vote and had few rights.

5) Give one example from the novel of a character in each of the following professions:
   a) the clergy   b) the military   c) the legal profession.

In-depth Questions

1) What evidence is there in *Pride and Prejudice* that there were big gaps between different social classes in England during the Regency Period?

2) How was travel during the Regency Period different to today?
   Why is this important in the novel?

3) Do you think Jane Austen agreed or disagreed with the practice of entailing estates away from women? Use quotes from the text to support your answer.

4) How does Austen show that the following characters think that they're superior to the professional classes or people 'in trade'?
   a) Lady Catherine de Bourgh   b) Caroline Bingley

5) What does Jane Austen's portrayal of the Gardiners and Miss Bingley suggest about Austen's own attitude to class?
   Use evidence from the text in your answer.

Analysis of Chapters 1 to 6 — The First Ball

OK, deep breath. Here we go. Fifteen pages' worth of tip-top plot analysis to impress the examiner with.

Austen uses dialogue to introduce her characters

Austen doesn't <u>describe</u> her characters much, so the reader has to form their <u>own opinions</u> from the <u>dialogue</u>. This helps to <u>develop</u> several aspects of the novel, for example:

- <u>Character</u> — Mrs Bennet comes across as <u>silly and annoying</u>. She's a <u>caricature</u> of a <u>pushy mother</u> — she wants to marry one of her daughters off to Mr Bingley before she's even <u>met</u> him because he's <u>rich</u>.

- <u>Themes</u> — the reader gets the impression that Mr and Mrs Bennet aren't <u>well-matched</u>. The <u>theme</u> of <u>unhappy relationships</u> and marrying someone for the <u>wrong reasons</u> is <u>developed</u> later in the novel.

You meet the two main couples

1) Austen <u>contrasts</u> the <u>personalities</u> of the novel's <u>two main couples</u> when they meet at the ball in Chapter 3.

- Bingley and Jane are <u>sweet</u> and <u>good-natured</u>, and they're <u>attracted</u> to each other straight away. The reader sees that they're <u>well-matched</u> and wants them to <u>end up together</u>, so the later events that threaten to separate them <u>add drama</u>.

- Elizabeth immediately <u>dislikes</u> Darcy and he's <u>indifferent</u> to her — it's an early introduction to the characters' <u>pride</u> and <u>prejudice</u>. Elizabeth's <u>snap judgement</u> about Darcy is really <u>important</u> — it <u>affects her view</u> for a lot of the novel and means that she doesn't <u>notice</u> when he starts to <u>admire</u> her.

Public opinion of Darcy changes from "great admiration" to "disgust" when he makes it clear he's not interested in marrying any of the local girls — Austen's criticising the shallowness and hypocrisy of society.

2) Bingley's sisters think Jane's "sweet". Because they <u>approve</u> of her, Bingley feels he can <u>pursue</u> her. Bingley's <u>reliance</u> on his sisters' opinion <u>foreshadows</u> the way he's <u>influenced</u> by Darcy later on.

Foreshadowing is when the writer hints at something that will happen later on in the novel.

3) Elizabeth and her friend Charlotte Lucas have <u>different opinions</u> on how Jane should act around Bingley. Elizabeth thinks she should just <u>be herself</u>, but Charlotte thinks that she should make her <u>feelings clear</u> by showing "more affection than she feels". Charlotte is proved <u>right</u> later in the novel when Darcy uses Jane's apparent <u>lack of interest</u> to split the couple up.

Theme — Marriage

Charlotte thinks that a <u>happy marriage</u> is "entirely a matter of chance". She believes that a relationship based on first impressions is just as likely to <u>succeed</u> as one based on <u>understanding</u> and <u>love</u>. Elizabeth represents a more <u>romantic</u> point of view — she claims Charlotte's opinion "is not sound".

© AF archive / Alamy

Make sure you don't mix up the Bennet sisters...

Here's a summary of all the Bennets. Eldest: Jane (pretty). Next: Elizabeth (heroine). Then: Mary (bookish). Nearly there: Kitty, who's called Catherine in the first few chapters. And finally: Lydia (oh, just you wait).

Analysis of Chapters 7 to 12 — At Netherfield

Mrs Bennet's scheming leads Jane to catch a cold, but Mr Bingley's definitely not giving her the cold shoulder.

A militia regiment arrives in Meryton

1) Kitty and Lydia are obsessed with the officers — it's all they talk about.

2) Mr Bennet calls his daughters "two of the silliest girls in the country" but he doesn't try to change them. Mrs Bennet says that Kitty and Lydia can't be expected "to have the sense of their father and mother" — this is ironic because Mrs Bennet's own lack of sense is what makes the girls so silly.

3) Mr and Mrs Bennet's responses highlight their flaws as parents.

Jane gets ill while she's visiting Netherfield

1) Jane catches a cold whilst visiting Netherfield and has to stay there — Elizabeth walks over to look after her.

2) Miss Bingley and Elizabeth act very differently around Mr Darcy. Miss Bingley is desperate for attention and constantly compliments him, whereas Elizabeth is witty and puts Darcy in his place.

3) The witty debates between Elizabeth and Darcy show how well-suited they are. Elizabeth isn't intimidated by Darcy's social status or wealth — she can hold her own with people who are socially superior to her.

Theme — Love

Darcy's attracted to Elizabeth rather than Miss Bingley. This suggests that Austen thinks personality is more important than status for a relationship.

Turning point in the action
Darcy starts to fall in love with Elizabeth.

Bingley's sisters make fun of the Bennets

1) Miss Bingley makes several attempts to put Darcy off Elizabeth:

- She makes fun of Elizabeth's "untidy" appearance and lack of "decorum" in front of Darcy, but it doesn't put him off — he thinks her eyes were "brightened by the exercise".

- She laughs at the Bennets' "low connections" but this also backfires — Bingley tells Miss Bingley that it doesn't make them "one jot less agreeable".

- When Mrs Bennet visits, Miss Bingley gives Darcy an "expressive smile" to draw his attention to Elizabeth's vulgar family.   *Vulgar means rude or improper.*

2) Miss Bingley's attempts to put Elizabeth down show her own ill-breeding, lack of manners and snobbery. Darcy and Bingley don't join in, which shows that they're nicer characters and have much better manners.

Writer's Techniques — Irony   *For more on irony, have a look at p.55.*

- Miss Bingley laughs at Mrs Bennet's bad manners and vulgarity, but can't see her own.

- She looks down on Elizabeth for having uncles in trade, but the Bingley fortune was made through trade.

"Her hair, so untidy, so blowsy!"

When Miss Bingley makes fun of Lizzy's appearance, Mr Darcy doesn't take the bait — but he does say her connections "materially lessen" her chances of a rich husband. Hindsight is a wonderful thing, eh Darcy?

Analysis of Chapters 13 to 16 — Mr Collins Visits

A new character to introduce to you here. It's Mr Collins — you're going to love him.

Mr Collins comes to stay

1) Mr Bennet announces his cousin, Mr Collins, is coming to visit. Mr Collins will inherit Longbourn, which could leave the Bennet women homeless.

© AF archive / Alamy

Women in Regency Society

Jane and Elizabeth's calm, dignified acceptance of the entailment highlights how unfair it is that the unpleasant, undeserving Mr Collins will inherit everything.

2) Mrs Bennet thinks he's "odious" and "hypocritical", and blames him for the entail. But she changes her mind when he hints that he wants to marry one of her daughters. Austen uses irony again — it's actually Mrs Bennet who is the hypocrite.

3) Mr Collins talks a lot about Lady Catherine. This highlights his snobbish obsession with social class and wealth.

Lady Catherine is Mr Collins's patron — she gave him the position of vicar (the "living") on her estate.

A sycophant is someone who sucks up to other people.

Character — Mr Collins

Even before Mr Collins shows up, his letter hints that he's pompous and sycophantic. The more intelligent characters like Elizabeth can tell straight away that he's an "oddity" and full of "self-importance". But the silly characters like Mary think his letter is "well expressed".

The Bennets meet a handsome new officer, Mr Wickham

KEY EVENT

1) Austen introduces Wickham positively — he's handsome and charming. This contrasts with how she introduces Darcy — Austen encourages the reader to like Wickham.

Writer's Techniques

When Darcy and Wickham bump into each other, one turns "white, the other red". Turning white is usually associated with shock or anger, going red suggests embarrassment. Austen deliberately doesn't say which character does what — this builds suspense about their past relationship.

Theme — Prejudice

Elizabeth is eager to believe Wickham's version of events because she likes him, and because she's already prejudiced against Darcy. Wickham increases Elizabeth's prejudices against Darcy and acts as an obstacle that prevents them from getting together.

2) Elizabeth finds Wickham attractive — Austen hints that he's a possible love interest.

3) Elizabeth is shocked and horrified when Wickham tells her his history with Darcy. She's doesn't like Darcy but she's still amazed that he's capable of such "malicious revenge". Their mutual dislike of Darcy brings them closer together.

4) Austen drops hints that Wickham shouldn't be trusted. For example, he checks how well Elizabeth knows Darcy before he tells his story, and seems concerned that Mr Collins knows Darcy's aunt, Lady Catherine. He also says he'll never "defy or expose" Darcy out of respect for his father — but that's exactly what he does.

EXAM TIP

Write about how Austen hints at characters' personalities...

Austen gives lots of clues about characters' personalities, other than what she tells you directly. You could comment on how all her silly characters get on well with each other — like Mrs Bennet, Lydia and Kitty.

Analysis of Chapters 17 to 18 — Netherfield Ball

These chapters are pretty important... ah yes, it's the much-anticipated Netherfield Ball, given by Mr Bingley.

Elizabeth guesses Mr Collins plans to propose

1) Mr Collins pays Elizabeth <u>extra attention</u> and she suspects he might propose.

2) She finds the idea of marrying Mr Collins <u>horrible</u>. She doesn't care that it would give her <u>financial stability</u> — she's <u>determined</u> to marry for <u>love</u>.

Elizabeth seems to be falling for Wickham

1) There's a ball at Netherfield and Elizabeth's <u>disappointed</u> that Wickham isn't there — Mr Denny tells her that Wickham "wished to avoid a certain gentleman". Elizabeth sees this as further proof of Wickham's <u>dignity</u>, rather than his <u>guilt</u>.

2) Miss Bingley tries to <u>warn</u> Elizabeth about Wickham, but Elizabeth <u>doesn't listen</u> because:

- She <u>doesn't like</u> Miss Bingley, so she doesn't <u>trust</u> her opinions.

- Miss Bingley comments on Wickham's "descent" and says "one could not expect much better" — this makes Elizabeth think it's Miss Bingley's <u>class prejudice</u> that makes her believe the <u>worst</u> of Wickham.

- Miss Bingley doesn't know any <u>details</u> — she's just <u>repeating</u> what she's heard from her brother.

Theme — Prejudice

When Elizabeth dances with Darcy she asks him whether he is "blinded by prejudice" — it's a <u>sly dig</u> about Wickham and another example of <u>irony</u> — Elizabeth is <u>criticising</u> Darcy's own prejudices without realising <u>her own</u>.

The irony is it's Elizabeth's own prejudice against Miss Bingley and her own feelings towards Wickham which affect her judgement.

But her feelings about Darcy are unclear

1) Darcy shows he's <u>overcoming</u> his prejudice when he asks Elizabeth to dance, but her prejudice is so <u>strong</u> that she doesn't <u>notice</u> how much <u>effort</u> he's making.

2) Austen drops various <u>hints</u> that Elizabeth <u>cares</u> more about Darcy's opinion than she <u>admits</u>:

- Elizabeth mentions Wickham and Darcy is visibly <u>shocked</u>. Elizabeth "could not go on" with the conversation — she doesn't want to make him <u>feel uncomfortable</u>.

- Elizabeth tries to <u>stop</u> Mr Collins introducing himself to Darcy — something considered <u>rude</u> by Regency standards. She doesn't want Mr Collins to <u>embarrass</u> her in front of Darcy.

- Mrs Bennet says in <u>earshot</u> of Darcy that she owes him no "particular civility" — Elizabeth tells her to be <u>quiet</u>, because she doesn't want to <u>offend</u> him.

© AF archive / Alamy

Theme — Social Class

Elizabeth is very <u>aware</u> of her family's <u>embarrassing behaviour</u> and how it might be <u>viewed</u> by <u>Mr Darcy</u>.

KEY QUOTE

"I shall... think of both gentlemen as I did before."

Lizzy ignores what Miss Bingley says about Darcy and Wickham because she thinks she's biased — Miss Bingley has only heard Darcy's side of the story. But Lizzy somehow forgets that <u>she's</u> only heard Wickham's.

Analysis of Chapters 19 to 23 — Mr Collins Proposes

Mr Collins wants a wife, Mr Collins wants a wife, eee aye addy-oh, Mr Collins wants a wife...

Mr Collins proposes to Elizabeth...

1) Mr Collins tells Elizabeth: "I singled you out as the companion of my future life". The reader sees the irony — Elizabeth was actually his second choice.

2) Elizabeth refuses. Although marrying Mr Collins would keep Longbourn in the Bennet family and offer them security, Elizabeth won't marry Mr Collins because she doesn't love him.

Character — Mr Collins

Mr Collins never says what he means — only what he thinks will make him look good or make other people like him. So when Elizabeth refuses him he assumes she's just saying no to show off her "delicacy" and increase his "suspense".

Theme — Marriage

Mr Collins's proposal shows a different view of marriage. He sees marriage as something expected of him by society and by Lady Catherine. He places this above his own "affection" for Elizabeth.

© AF archive / Alamy

...and is finally accepted by Charlotte

1) Charlotte is prepared to marry for financial security rather than love, so when she's happy to spend time with Mr Collins it makes the reader suspect that she's trying to attract a proposal. Elizabeth doesn't realise this and thinks Charlotte's just being kind — this adds dramatic irony.

Women in Regency Society

- Charlotte is twenty-seven — quite old to be single by Regency standards. Marrying Mr Collins will give her financial security and independence from her parents.
- People often had to marry for practical reasons rather than love.

2) Mr Collins proposes to Charlotte — his second proposal in three days. He's determined to get married and doesn't care who to.

3) Elizabeth is shocked that Charlotte accepts — she can't believe that someone would marry purely for practical reasons, without having any affection for the other person.

4) Elizabeth believes it's impossible for Charlotte to be even "tolerably happy" — this emphasises Austen's views about the importance of marrying for love, not just for money.

Bingley leaves Netherfield

1) Jane gets a letter from Miss Bingley telling her that they have left Netherfield. She says that Mr Bingley plans to spend the winter in London, and is expected to marry Darcy's sister.

2) The letter increases Elizabeth's prejudice against Miss Bingley and Mr Darcy — she rightly assumes that they are trying to split up Jane and Bingley.

"Nobody can tell what I suffer!"

Mrs Bennet is hilarious in these chapters — she's so melodramatic, especially after Lizzy turns down Mr Collins's proposal. You could write about how Austen uses her to satirise Regency society (see p.55 for more).

Analysis of Chapters 24 to 27 — Jane Goes to London

These are some eventful chapters coming up, so brace yourself. It's all go.

The Gardiners are Elizabeth's most sensible relations

1) The Gardiners visit Longbourn and see how <u>unhappy</u> Jane is about Bingley leaving Netherfield. They <u>invite</u> her to <u>London</u> — they're <u>kind</u> and have Jane's <u>best interests</u> at heart.

> **Character — Mr Bennet**
>
> Mr Bennet <u>doesn't care</u> about Jane's <u>heartbreak</u>. This foreshadows his <u>unsympathetic</u> behaviour towards Lydia in later chapters.

2) Austen <u>contrasts</u> the Gardiners's <u>behaviour</u> with that of the Bennets. Mrs Bennet talks <u>endlessly</u> about Bingley and Mr Bennet <u>jokes</u> about Jane being "crossed in love" — this highlights their <u>inadequacy</u> as parents and their <u>insensitivity</u>.

3) Mrs Gardiner warns Elizabeth about Wickham — she describes the match as "<u>imprudent</u>" (a bad idea) because Wickham <u>isn't rich</u>. Elizabeth's reply that she "will not be in a hurry" shows that she's aware that she needs to consider <u>practical matters</u> when marrying. However, she <u>won't promise</u> not to marry Wickham — she still thinks <u>love</u> is <u>more important</u> than money.

Mr Wickham is in it for the money

1) Wickham's lost interest in Elizabeth and is now <u>pursuing</u> Miss King — who's just inherited £10,000.

© Focus/Everett/Rex Features

2) Mrs Gardiner thinks Wickham's behaviour is "mercenary" (he's after money) but Elizabeth disagrees — she thinks it's "prudent". It's <u>ironic</u> that Elizabeth <u>judges</u> Charlotte for marrying for <u>money</u>, but not Wickham.

> **Theme — Prejudice**
>
> The reader gets the impression that Elizabeth might be a <u>bad judge</u> of character — she's too <u>blinded</u> by Wickham's <u>charm</u> to see his <u>flaws</u>. This suggests that some of her <u>judgements</u> about <u>other characters</u> might also be <u>wrong</u>.

Letters drive the plot forward

See p.58 for more on letters.

1) Austen uses Elizabeth's letters from Jane and Charlotte to <u>develop the plot</u>.

2) Jane's letters show Miss Bingley's <u>true nature</u> — she's <u>rude</u> and makes it clear she doesn't want to see Jane.

3) Charlotte's letters are <u>reserved</u> and she "mentioned nothing which she could not praise". Charlotte wants to prove Elizabeth <u>wrong</u> about her marriage to Mr Collins.

> **Theme — Social Class**
>
> Austen contrasts the Gardiners' <u>kindness</u> and <u>sensitivity</u> towards Jane with Miss Bingley's behaviour — she's so rude to Jane that Jane believes herself to be "entirely deceived in Miss Bingley's regard for me". This shows that <u>intelligence</u> and <u>good manners</u> are not a matter of <u>class</u>.

EXAM TIP

Mention Austen's use of letters...

Some information is given to the reader through letters, which is a different <u>form</u> to the rest of the novel. There are marks for form, structure and language in your exam, so make sure you've revised all three.

Analysis of Chapters 28 to 29 — Elizabeth Visits Kent

Elizabeth's off to stay with Mr Collins and meet Lady Catherine. Rather her than me...

Elizabeth visits Mr and Mrs Collins

1) Jane Austen uses Charlotte's marriage to <u>show</u> that marrying for money <u>doesn't</u> lead to <u>happiness</u>.

- Elizabeth notes that Charlotte "wisely did not hear" her husband's speeches — she <u>deliberately ignores</u> him.
- Charlotte encourages Mr Collins to spend time in the garden "as much as possible" — she doesn't want to <u>spend time</u> with him.

Writer's Techniques — Plot

Elizabeth's trip to Hunsford keeps the reader interested by changing the <u>setting</u> and introducing <u>new characters</u>. It also gives Elizabeth the chance to meet Darcy again.

Character — Mr Collins

Mr Collins is <u>materialistic</u>. He talks about Lady Catherine's <u>possessions</u> — "so many servants", "so splendid a dinner" and "such rooms". His focus on wealth shows that he's <u>not</u> really suited to his <u>job</u>.

2) Despite her indifference towards her <u>husband</u>, Charlotte is <u>satisfied</u> with her <u>life</u>. Once Elizabeth sees Charlotte's "cheerful" air and "contentment" she sees the <u>advantages</u> of the marriage and is <u>more positive</u> about it. This shows that Elizabeth is <u>developing</u> as a character — she's not <u>fixated</u> on her original beliefs.

3) Charlotte's marriage has some <u>similarities</u> to the Bennets' — both Charlotte and Mr Bennet have to suffer the <u>silliness</u> and <u>self-absorption</u> of their partners. However, unlike Mr Bennet, Charlotte treats her partner with respect and never <u>mocks</u> him.

The group visits Lady Catherine

Language — Lady Catherine

The conversation is <u>dominated</u> by Lady Catherine. She asks lots of questions but gives <u>little chance</u> for the others to answer. This shows that she's only interested in her <u>own views</u> and doesn't think that anyone else has anything <u>worth saying</u>.

1) Lady Catherine is <u>rude</u> and <u>arrogant</u> — Elizabeth feels the "impertinence" of Lady Catherine's questions but answers "very composedly". Again, this shows that <u>wealth</u> and <u>status</u> aren't a guarantee of <u>good breeding</u>. Elizabeth is more <u>polite</u> and <u>well-mannered</u> than Lady Catherine.

2) Lady Catherine is a <u>caricature</u> who highlights all the <u>worst traits</u> of the aristocracy. She "likes to have the distinction of rank preserved" and is "gratified" by Mr Collins and Sir Lucas's ridiculous flattery.

Character — Elizabeth Bennet

Apart from her first impressions of Darcy and Wickham, Elizabeth's quite a good <u>judge of character</u> — she can see through characters like Miss Bingley, Mr Collins and Lady Catherine.

3) Lady Catherine is <u>shocked</u> when Elizabeth stands up to her: "you give your opinion very decidedly". This <u>clash</u> of personalities <u>foreshadows</u> Lady Catherine and Elizabeth's <u>disagreement</u> later.

© AF archive / Alamy

KEY QUOTE *"she was not used to have her judgement controverted."*

Lady Catherine is rich with a high social rank, but she hasn't got any manners and isn't a very nice person. Lizzy, who she sees as inferior, is ten times the person she is. Turns out money and titles aren't everything.

Analysis of Chapters 30 to 33 — Darcy Returns

Mr Darcy turns up at Rosings while Elizabeth is staying with the Collinses. Coincidence? I think not.

Colonel Fitzwilliam is a potential love interest

1) Colonel Fitzwilliam (Darcy's cousin) comes with Darcy to visit Lady Catherine — everyone <u>likes</u> him, he's "truly the gentleman".

2) Colonel Fitzwilliam and Elizabeth <u>get on</u> straight away, and she "caught his fancy very much". However, it's soon clear that <u>nothing</u> will happen — he admits he has to marry with "some attention to money", so Elizabeth isn't <u>wealthy</u> enough for him.

> **Theme — Marriage**
>
> Although he comes from a <u>wealthy</u> family, Colonel Fitzwilliam <u>isn't rich</u> — inheritance laws mean that the family estate will pass to his brother. He shows that it's not just women who have to marry for <u>financial security</u>.

Mr Darcy is still in love with Elizabeth

1) There are lots of <u>hints</u> that Darcy's in love with Elizabeth:

- When Darcy arrives at Rosings he visits Elizabeth <u>straight away</u>.

- When Elizabeth chats to Colonel Fitzwilliam, Darcy's <u>attentive</u> — he "repeatedly turned towards them with a look of curiosity".

- Elizabeth keeps <u>bumping</u> into him on her walks — he's hanging around her favourite routes because he <u>wants to see her</u>.

© AF archive / Alamy

2) Darcy admits he has a problem "conversing easily" — this suggests that Elizabeth has misjudged his <u>shyness</u> as <u>pride</u> and makes the reader <u>sympathise</u> with him.

3) Darcy and Elizabeth seem to be getting on <u>well</u> — they have more <u>witty debates</u> and he makes an effort to get to know her. The reader <u>warms</u> to him but Elizabeth is still <u>prejudiced</u> against him.

4) Her prejudice <u>increases</u> when Colonel Fitzwilliam tells her that Darcy broke up Bingley and Jane. By revealing this, Colonel Fitzwilliam creates another <u>obstacle</u> that Darcy and Elizabeth have to overcome.

Lady Catherine embarrasses her nephews

Elizabeth continues to visit Lady Catherine with Mr and Mrs Collins. Austen uses the character of Lady Catherine to <u>criticise snobbery</u> and <u>class prejudices</u> — although she's <u>rich</u> and <u>powerful</u>, she's also <u>vulgar</u> and <u>rude</u>.

> **Theme — Social Class**
>
> Darcy is "ashamed" of his Aunt's "ill-breeding" and Colonel Fitzwilliam tries to "avoid a reply" to her questions. This is another example of <u>irony</u> — Darcy is put off by Elizabeth's <u>embarrassing family</u>, but his isn't much better — they've just got <u>more money</u>.

- Lady Catherine's <u>arrogant</u> — she tells the room she would have been "a great proficient" at the piano if she'd learnt.

- She's <u>superficial</u> — she finds the company of Elizabeth and the Collinses "acceptable" only when she can get "nobody else".

- She's <u>rude</u> — she <u>criticises</u> Elizabeth's piano playing and says that her taste is "not equal to Anne's."

EXAM TIP

Talk about how Austen hints at Darcy's feelings...

Mr Darcy is turning up on Lizzy's doorstep, following her about the countryside and watching her whenever she chats to another man. You can say that Austen slowly builds up to the idea that he has feelings for her.

Analysis of Chapters 34 to 36 — Darcy Proposes

Finally, someone other than Mr Collins proposes. Darcy makes a bit of a mess of it though.

Darcy reveals his feelings and proposes

The full extent of Darcy and Elizabeth's <u>pride</u> and <u>prejudice</u> is revealed when Darcy proposes.

1) Darcy's <u>pride</u> in his <u>wealth</u>, <u>social status</u> and <u>character</u> means that he has "no doubt of a favourable answer". He thinks he's such a <u>good catch</u> Elizabeth couldn't possibly <u>refuse</u>.

2) His proposal also shows how deep his <u>class prejudice</u> runs — he talks about Elizabeth's family as "obstacles" and how he's tried to "conquer" his feelings.

Language — Mr Darcy

Austen <u>contrasts</u> Darcy's proposal with Mr Collins's — Darcy tells Elizabeth he "ardently" <u>admires</u> and <u>loves</u> her, whereas Mr Collins doesn't mention love at all. Darcy's proposal seems more <u>genuine</u>.

Theme — Marriage

Darcy's a <u>rich</u> man from a <u>powerful family</u> — by turning him down, Elizabeth proves again that she's not interested in marrying for <u>money</u>.

3) Darcy hurts Elizabeth's <u>pride</u> when he insults her family, so she replies rudely, "if I could *feel* gratitude, I would now thank you".

4) In her anger, Elizabeth reveals the causes of her <u>prejudice</u> against Darcy — the <u>stories</u> she's heard from Wickham and Colonel Fitzwilliam. In this way, Austen gives Darcy an opportunity to reveal the <u>truth</u> and move his relationship with Elizabeth <u>forward</u>.

For more on the theme of love and Austen's views on listening to the head and the heart have a look at p.43.

Theme — Love

Darcy talks about Elizabeth's "inferiority" — he still feels that she's <u>beneath</u> him socially. He's listening to his <u>heart</u> but not his <u>head</u> — he needs to feel that marrying Elizabeth is a <u>sensible choice</u> as well as a <u>romantic</u> one before he can really be <u>happy</u>.

Darcy's letter to Elizabeth explains his actions

Turning point in the action
Elizabeth realises she's been wrong about Darcy.

1) Darcy gives Elizabeth a <u>letter</u> explaining <u>why</u> he broke Jane and Bingley up, and <u>why</u> he hates Wickham.

2) Darcy's letter <u>explains</u> his side of things and helps both characters <u>overcome</u> their <u>pride</u> and <u>prejudice</u>:

- By revealing Georgiana's near-elopement, Darcy puts his <u>pride</u> to one side — this shows how <u>strong</u> his need to <u>explain</u> himself is.

- Elizabeth starts to realise that her <u>prejudices</u> about Darcy are based on what Wickham has told her and that she's been <u>misled</u> by Wickham's charm. She's also forced to <u>accept</u> that Darcy's <u>criticisms</u> of her family were <u>fair</u> and that Jane's feelings were "little displayed".

- Elizabeth's pride is <u>humbled</u> — she realises that she's not as good a judge of character as she thought and she's been "wretchedly blind".

© AF archive / Alamy

KEY QUOTE

"you chose to tell me that you liked me against your will"

Poor Elizabeth — first Mr Collins's shambles of a proposal, now this. Darcy's just being honest, but 'I've tried so hard not to love you' isn't really what you want to hear, is it? Maybe say it with flowers next time, Darce...

Analysis of Chapters 37 to 41 — Back to Longbourn

Darcy and Fitzwilliam toddle off and Lizzy heads back to Meryton.

Austen uses irony and humour to lighten the mood

1) Elizabeth leaves Kent and travels back to Longbourn. She meets Jane, Kitty and Lydia on the way.

2) After the serious events of the previous chapters, Austen uses irony and silly characters like Lydia to give a bit of light relief.

- Lady Catherine thinks Darcy's "acutely" upset because he doesn't want to leave Rosings — Elizabeth, and the reader, know he's actually upset about Elizabeth's rejection.

- Mr Collins tells Elizabeth that he thinks he and Charlotte are "designed for each other" — he's completely unaware that his wife tries to distance herself from him as much as possible.

- Lydia's silliness sets a comic tone — she wants to treat her sisters to lunch but they have to lend her the money — she's spent all hers on a "ugly" hat. This reminds the reader of her reckless behaviour and sets up the events to come.

© TopFoto

Lydia boasts about her adventures with the militia and talks about getting married — this foreshadows the scandal she's about to cause.

Lydia goes to Brighton, against Elizabeth's better judgement

1) Back at Longbourn, the Bennet family aren't very happy. Mrs Bennet is still upset about Bingley moving to London, and Lydia and Kitty are heartbroken that the militia are leaving Meryton.

Theme — Love

Austen contrasts the behaviour of Elizabeth and Lydia. Elizabeth doesn't pursue Darcy, whereas Lydia follows Wickham and the officers to Brighton to get their attention. This shows the difference in maturity of the two girls.

2) Darcy's letter has made Elizabeth very sensitive to her family's bad behaviour and she feels the "justice" of his comments as she watches how they act.

Writer's Techniques

Elizabeth warns Mr Bennet that Lydia's behaviour is damaging the family's "respectability". This foreshadows the danger to the family's reputation when Lydia and Wickham elope.

3) Mr Bennet's flaws as a parent are highlighted when he agrees to let Lydia go to Brighton, despite Elizabeth's warning — he only cares that he "shall have no peace" if he doesn't let her go. He treats it all as a joke — he sees the flaws in Lydia's character but he won't do anything to fix them.

Theme — Reputation

Jane and Elizabeth decide to not mention the truth about Wickham to anyone — they don't want to ruin his reputation. This choice has serious consequences.

4) Elizabeth bumps into Wickham — their conversation shows how her opinion of him has totally changed. She defends Darcy and feels a "disgust" for Wickham that hints that her feelings for Darcy are getting stronger.

 KEY QUOTE *"We shall have no peace... if Lydia does not go to Brighton."*
Mr Bennet doesn't care that Lydia's off to Brighton to flirt with "at least six officers at once", as long as he gets some peace and quiet — he thinks she can't turn out worse than she already is. Oh, if only he knew...

Analysis of Chapters 42 to 45 — At Pemberley

Elizabeth goes on holiday with the Gardiners — they happen to visit Pemberley, home to a certain Mr Darcy...

Elizabeth's feelings towards Darcy grow stronger

1) Elizabeth is "delighted" by Darcy's home, and wonders what it would be like to be "mistress of Pemberley" — she's starting to see Darcy as a <u>possible husband</u>.

2) Elizabeth meets Darcy's housekeeper, Mrs Reynolds. She's "less fine" and "more civil" than Elizabeth expects — this hints that Darcy <u>dislikes grandeur</u> and <u>affected manners</u>, and chooses the people he wants around him on the basis of <u>personality</u>.

3) Mrs Reynolds only has <u>good</u> things to say about Darcy — he's "affable to the poor" and she's "never had a cross word from him". Elizabeth realises the "praise of an intelligent servant" is likely to give an <u>accurate picture</u> — if Darcy had been really <u>snobbish</u>, he'd have treated his servants <u>badly</u>.

Pemberley represents Darcy himself — see p.57.

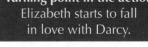

Theme — Pride

Mrs Reynolds suggests that Darcy is <u>proud</u>, but in a different way than Elizabeth first thought. He has <u>pride</u> in his <u>estate</u> and looks after his <u>tenants</u>.

Turning point in the action
Elizabeth starts to fall in love with Darcy.

Darcy is the perfect gentleman

1) Darcy turns up at Pemberley — Elizabeth's <u>embarrassed</u> that he'll think she's "purposely thrown herself in his way", but he's <u>friendly</u> and <u>welcoming</u>.

2) He asks to be introduced to the Gardiners. Elizabeth expects him to look down on them because of their class, but he's <u>charming</u> and <u>polite</u> — this shows that he has <u>overcome</u> his class prejudices. Elizabeth can't believe that he is "so altered", and wants to believe it's for <u>her sake</u>.

Writer's Techniques

Darcy still seems interested in Elizabeth — the reader <u>expects</u> that he might <u>propose</u> to Elizabeth again and she might say 'yes'. This <u>expectation</u> makes the events which threaten the couple's happiness even more <u>dramatic</u>.

3) Elizabeth feels <u>awkward</u> around him — she "scarcely dared lift her eyes to his face". This shows how <u>strong</u> her feelings for Darcy have grown.

Writer's Techniques

The Gardiners are presented as <u>intelligent</u> and <u>sensible</u>, so the reader trusts their <u>good opinion</u> of Darcy.

4) Darcy wants to <u>introduce</u> Elizabeth to his sister Georgiana. Elizabeth is "anxious" about meeting her — the reader sees that she's actually <u>worried</u> about <u>impressing</u> Darcy. Elizabeth's <u>eagerness</u> to like and be liked by Georgiana show that she's <u>overcome</u> her <u>prejudice</u> against Darcy's family now.

5) Elizabeth visits Pemberley and finds Miss Bingley there — it's clear that she's still <u>jealous</u> about Darcy's feelings for Elizabeth. She makes a <u>sly dig</u> about Wickham to try and embarrass Elizabeth in front of Darcy, but it <u>backfires</u> — she <u>embarrasses</u> Georgiana and highlights her own <u>lack of manners</u>.

KEY QUOTE

"Her keenest attention was awakened"

Elizabeth's opinions of Darcy are changing, and she's keen to find out more about him. She doesn't actually want to see him at Pemberley, though. Rejecting him, then randomly appearing at his house... bit awkward.

Analysis of Chapters 46 to 49 — Lydia Elopes

Just as things are starting to look up for Elizabeth and Darcy, Lydia goes and ruins it all.

Elizabeth finds out that Lydia has eloped with Wickham

1) Elizabeth gets a letter from Jane saying that Lydia has <u>run off</u> with Wickham — this news is used to <u>change the course of the action</u>. For more on Austen's use of letters, have a look at p.58.

2) Elizabeth tells Darcy what's happened — the fact that she tells him about such a <u>private</u> family matter shows how much she <u>trusts</u> him. However, she's convinced that Darcy won't want to be associated with the <u>scandal</u>.

3) It's <u>ironic</u> that Elizabeth realises that she loves Darcy only when she thinks she's <u>lost him</u>.

4) The <u>pace</u> of these chapters <u>speeds up dramatically</u> — a lot happens in a <u>short</u> space of time. This adds <u>drama</u>.

© AF archive / Alamy

Turning point in the action
Lydia elopes and threatens the Bennets' reputation.

Theme — Reputation
It's not just <u>Lydia's</u> reputation that's threatened by her elopement — her "disgrace" will <u>damage</u> all the Bennet sisters' <u>reputations</u> and make it <u>harder</u> for them to marry <u>well</u>.

The scandal highlights the Bennets' weaknesses

1) Austen once again <u>contrasts</u> the <u>parenting abilities</u> of the Bennets and the Gardiners. Mr and Mrs Gardiner are calm and reasonable and try to <u>reassure</u> Elizabeth that Wickham will marry Lydia.

2) In contrast, Mrs Bennet's behaviour highlights her <u>stupidity</u> and <u>weakness</u> as a parent:

- She won't leave her room and <u>complains</u> about her own "sufferings and ill-usage". She <u>accuses</u> the Forsters of "great neglect" — it's ironic since it's her neglect of parental duty that made Lydia so <u>wild</u>.

- It also shows the <u>hysterical</u> side of her character — she thinks Mr Bennet will fight Wickham and be killed.

- Mrs Bennet doesn't <u>learn</u> anything from the situation — when she hears that Lydia and Wickham are getting married all she can think about are <u>wedding clothes</u>. She doesn't care that Lydia's marrying a scoundrel who's brought <u>shame</u> on the family — she's just <u>delighted</u> that her daughter is getting <u>married</u>.

3) Mr Bennet's behaviour also reveals his <u>flaws</u>:

- He goes to London to find Lydia and Wickham, but comes back <u>early</u> even though he <u>hasn't</u> found them.

- He leaves Mr Gardiner to <u>find</u> the couple and apparently <u>pay</u> Wickham off.

In Chapter 48 he tells Kitty that he's "learnt to be cautious", but we don't see much evidence that his approach to parenting has actually <u>changed</u>.

4) Austen uses a <u>letter</u> to reveal Lydia's thoughts — she sees the whole thing as <u>funny</u>: "what a good joke it will be". This shows Lydia's <u>immaturity</u> — she doesn't realise the <u>consequences</u> of her actions.

Talk about how the pace of the novel changes...

It's all happening — Lydia's gone off with Wickham, Elizabeth's realised she loves Darcy, and the reputation of the family is at stake. Show the examiner that you understand how this change of pace creates tension.

Analysis of Chapters 50 to 55 — Bingley Proposes

We've been waiting for it since Chapter Three — Bingers finally gets down on one knee...

Elizabeth realises she's in love with Darcy

1) Elizabeth <u>regrets</u> telling Darcy about the elopement — this is <u>ironic</u>, since it was him who <u>saved</u> Lydia from the scandal.

2) Elizabeth admits she "confidently depended" on Darcy's <u>secrecy</u> — she's beginning to see him in a <u>new light</u> and notice his <u>strengths</u>.

> **Writer's Techniques**
>
> Lydia's elopement <u>forces</u> Elizabeth and Darcy <u>apart</u> — this makes the <u>climax</u> of the novel more <u>dramatic</u>.

> **Theme — Marriage**
>
> Lydia and Wickham visit Longbourn — neither of them seem <u>ashamed</u> of what's happened and they haven't <u>learned</u> anything from their actions. Already, Wickham's affection is "not equal to Lydia's" — Austen is <u>warning</u> her readers what happens if you marry for the <u>wrong reasons</u>.

3) Although Elizabeth realises that Darcy is the man who would "most suit her", she thinks he must have <u>lost interest</u> because of the scandal and her family's <u>connection</u> with Wickham.

4) Austen <u>encourages</u> the reader to think that Darcy's <u>lost interest</u> through Elizabeth's <u>language</u> — she repeats that his feelings couldn't "survive such a blow as this", that there was now a "gulf impassable between them" and that it was "no longer likely they should meet". This sets up the <u>final twist</u> and make their <u>union</u> more <u>dramatic</u>.

5) Elizabeth discovers it was Darcy who <u>paid off</u> Wickham — this hints that his feelings for her <u>haven't changed</u>. Getting involved in Lydia's silliness shows that Darcy has <u>overcome</u> his <u>pride</u> for Elizabeth's sake.

Bingley proposes to Jane

 KEY EVENT

1) Bingley returns to Netherfield. Mrs Bennet proclaims "I am sure I never want to see him again", but then tells Mr Bennet that he must pay Bingley a <u>visit</u> — it's another example of her <u>hypocrisy</u>.

2) Darcy visits Longbourn and Elizabeth's very <u>awkward</u> around him — she's <u>different</u> from the <u>self-confident</u>, <u>witty</u> Elizabeth the reader sees in <u>earlier chapters</u>. This <u>change</u> in behaviour shows how her feelings towards Darcy have <u>altered</u> — she's more aware of how he <u>sees</u> her and of her family's <u>inappropriate behaviour</u>.

3) Bingley <u>proposes</u> to Jane — Darcy has <u>encouraged</u> his friend to marry Jane <u>despite</u> her family connections. This suggests that Darcy has <u>overcome his prejudice</u> against the Bennets — one of the <u>obstacles</u> between him and Elizabeth, and hints that he might soon <u>propose again</u>.

> **Writer's Techniques**
>
> Mr Darcy is <u>reserved</u> too — it's an example of how Austen portrays her characters as more <u>restricted</u> when they're <u>indoors</u>. For more on this, turn to p.57.

© WORKING TITLE / THE KOBAL COLLECTION

> **Theme — Marriage**
>
> Elizabeth thinks that Bingley's love for Jane is "rationally founded". This suggests that he's marrying her for the <u>right reasons</u> — <u>love</u> and <u>compatibility</u>, rather than <u>money</u> or <u>status</u>.

EXAM TIP

Write about Mrs Bennet's fickle nature...

You could discuss what Mrs Bennet's reaction to Jane's engagement shows about her character. She quickly forgets all of her excitement about Lydia's marriage — Jane's now become her "favourite child". Bit fickle.

Analysis of Chapters 56 to 57 — Lady Catherine Visits

Lady C turns up and meddles in Elizabeth's affairs — are Darcy and Elizabeth over before they've even begun?

Lady Catherine gives Elizabeth a piece of her mind

1) Lady Catherine arrives <u>unannounced</u> at Longbourn and is <u>rude</u> to the Bennets — she tells them their sitting room is "inconvenient" and their park is "very small". She thinks the Bennets are <u>beneath her</u>.

2) Mrs Bennet is "flattered", despite Lady Catherine's <u>rudeness</u> and describes her as "civil". Mrs Bennet is <u>blinded</u> by Lady Catherine's <u>status</u> and can't see how <u>rude</u> and <u>unpleasant</u> she really is.

Writer's Techniques — Irony

It's <u>ironic</u> that Lady Catherine tries to <u>prevent</u> Darcy and Elizabeth's marriage, but actually ends up bringing them together.

Theme — Marriage

Lady Catherine wants Darcy to marry her daughter, Anne. Austen hints that she doesn't agree with <u>arranged marriages</u> by suggesting that Darcy and Anne would be a <u>bad match</u>.

3) Lady Catherine tells Elizabeth she can't marry Darcy because she's <u>socially inferior</u> to him — Lady Catherine expects to <u>prevent</u> the marriage. She's another <u>obstacle</u> that they have to <u>overcome</u>.

4) The <u>dialogue</u> between Lady Catherine and Elizabeth is <u>dramatic</u>. Lady Catherine is <u>rude</u> and outspoken, but Elizabeth is very <u>dignified</u>. Austen shows that pride can be a <u>good</u> thing — Elizabeth's <u>pride</u> in herself lets her <u>stand up</u> to Lady Catherine.

Writer's Techniques

Lady Catherine and Elizabeth talk more <u>freely</u> when they're <u>outside</u> — Lady Catherine is <u>rude</u> to Elizabeth, calling her an "Unfeeling, selfish girl!" Elizabeth also speaks <u>freely</u>, though <u>unlike</u> Lady Catherine she's <u>polite</u>, e.g. telling Lady Catherine "*you* may ask questions which *I* shall not choose to answer."

Mr Collins sends another helpful letter

1) Mr Collins writes to advise Elizabeth <u>not to accept</u> Darcy's <u>proposal</u>.

2) Mr Bennet <u>laughs</u> at the thought of Elizabeth marrying Darcy — he "probably never looked at *you* in his life!" This shows how <u>insensitive</u> Mr Bennet can be.

3) Mr Bennet also comments on Elizabeth's "pointed dislike" of Darcy. This makes Elizabeth <u>regret</u> her earlier <u>prejudice</u> and the things she said about Darcy — Austen is showing that <u>blind prejudice</u> has <u>negative results</u>.

4) Mr Collins tells Mr Bennet that he should <u>forgive</u> Wickham and Lydia but "never to admit them in your sight, or allow their names to be mentioned in your hearing".

© AF archive / Alamy

Character — Mr Collins

This is further evidence that Mr Collins isn't a good Christian — he's <u>hypocritical</u> and <u>unforgiving</u>.

KEY QUOTE

"Are the shades of Pemberley to be thus polluted?"

Lots of characters think that a marriage between Elizabeth and Darcy is a terrible idea — none more so than Lady Catherine. Elizabeth would've agreed with them before, but now she's regretting her earlier prejudices.

Analysis of Chapters 58 to 61 — Darcy Proposes

Everything is starting to fall into place at last for Elizabeth and Darcy. Where are my tissues...

Darcy and Lizzy have overcome all obstacles to their marriage

1) Darcy and Elizabeth go for a <u>walk</u> — and he <u>proposes</u> again.

2) Darcy talks about his "respect" for Elizabeth's family. This shows how he's <u>put aside</u> his <u>prejudices</u> about the Bennets — the main <u>obstacle</u> to their marriage.

KEY EVENT

3) Austen shows how much Elizabeth and Darcy have <u>developed</u>:

© Moviestore Collection Ltd

- Darcy says Elizabeth's criticisms "tortured" him but he admits their "justice" and sees that he <u>needed</u> to <u>overcome</u> his class prejudice and feeling of <u>superiority</u>.

- Elizabeth <u>regrets</u> that she allowed her initial prejudice against Darcy to blind her to the truth, and is <u>ashamed</u> that she abused him "so abominably" when he first proposed.

Writer's Techniques

Austen doesn't write about Darcy's second proposal in much detail — she focuses on the proposals that go <u>wrong</u>. This is because the unsuccessful proposals create <u>humour</u> (Mr Collins's proposal), or add <u>drama</u> (Mr Darcy's first attempt).

4) Austen suggests that their relationship makes them into <u>better people</u>, and because of this they emerge as the <u>happiest</u> couple in the novel.

The novel has a happy ending, but some things don't change

1) The ending of *Pride and Prejudice* encourages the reader to think that being able to <u>recognise</u> and <u>overcome</u> your <u>flaws</u> leads to <u>happiness</u>.

2) Austen shows how Jane and Elizabeth's happy marriages <u>positively affect</u> the other characters:

- <u>Kitty</u> spends more time with Jane and Elizabeth and becomes "less ignorant and less insipid".

- <u>Mary</u> isn't <u>overshadowed</u> by her sisters any more and becomes more <u>sociable</u>.

- Elizabeth teaches <u>Georgiana</u> to be more <u>confident</u> and sets a <u>good example</u> of a happy marriage.

3) However, Austen suggests that the characters who <u>can't</u> see their own <u>faults</u> are <u>unable to change</u>. Lydia and Wickham's marriage has "sunk into indifference". Similarly, Miss Bingley remains "almost as attentive" to Darcy and has "paid off every arrear of civility" to Elizabeth — she's just as <u>fake</u> as ever.

Themes — Social Class

The novel <u>ends</u> with the <u>Gardiners</u>, and credits them with "uniting" Darcy and Elizabeth. The Gardiners are responsible for the happy ending, despite being <u>looked down on</u> by other characters because of their <u>class</u>. In contrast, some of the upper-class characters tried to <u>separate</u> Elizabeth and Darcy. This reinforces Austen's message that <u>wealth</u> and <u>status</u> don't make someone a <u>better person</u>.

EXAM TIP

Write about the changes in Elizabeth and Darcy...

Impress the examiner by explaining that Darcy and Lizzy have become better people — they've overcome their prejudice towards one another, which was one of the main obstacles to their marriage. Lovely stuff.

Practice Questions

Well, I'm feeling a bit exhausted after all that — 'Pride and Prejudice' covers more than a year and it's a pretty eventful one too. Best to check you've taken it all in with these questions.

Quick Questions

1) Why does Jane have to stay at Netherfield in Chapter Seven?

2) Why doesn't Elizabeth listen to Miss Bingley's warning about Wickham?

3) Find an example from the text that suggests how Charlotte Lucas feels about Mr Collins after her marriage.

4) Why does Wickham suddenly lose interest in Elizabeth in Chapter 26?

5) Why does Lady Catherine visit Elizabeth at Longbourn?

6) Find a quote from the text to support the view that Lydia hasn't changed by the end of the novel.

In-depth Questions

1) Look at the following quote from Miss Caroline Bingley:

   "I have an excessive regard for Miss Jane Bennet, she is really a very sweet girl, and I wish with all my heart she were well settled."

   Do you think Miss Bingley really means what she says here? Use evidence from Chapters 7–12 of the novel to help you explain your answer.

2) The reactions of Darcy and Wickham to their meeting in Chapter 15 are described as follows: "Both changed colour, one looked white, the other red."
   Why do you think Austen doesn't tell the reader which was which?

3) How does Darcy's letter in Chapter 35 change Elizabeth's feelings towards him?

4) Does Lydia's elopement come as a surprise to the reader? Explain your answer.

Practice Questions

Your brain should be nicely warmed up after those questions, so it's time for some exam-style questions. Don't tackle them all at once — pick one that takes your fancy and try and do it in exam-style conditions. Take a break, then have a look at what you've written and use this book to try to improve your answer. You don't need to write a full essay for all of these questions — just coming up with a plan can be really useful.

Exam-style Questions

1) Use this extract to answer the question that follows.

> "I see what you are feeling," replied Charlotte. "You must be surprised, very much surprised—so lately as Mr. Collins was wishing to marry you. But when you have had time to think it all over, I hope you will be satisfied with what I have done. I am not romantic, you know. I never was. I ask only a comfortable home; and considering Mr. Collins's character, connections, and situation in life, I am convinced that my chance of happiness with him is as fair as most people can boast on entering the marriage state."
>
> Elizabeth quietly answered "Undoubtedly;" and after an awkward pause, they returned to the rest of the family. Charlotte did not stay much longer, and Elizabeth was then left to reflect on what she had heard. It was a long time before she became at all reconciled to the idea of so unsuitable a match. The strangeness of Mr. Collins's making two offers of marriage within three days was nothing in comparison of his being now accepted. She had always felt that Charlotte's opinion of matrimony was not exactly like her own, but she could not have supposed it possible that, when called into action, she would have sacrificed every better feeling to worldly advantage. Charlotte the wife of Mr. Collins was a most humiliating picture! And to the pang of a friend disgracing herself and sunk in her esteem, was added the distressing conviction that it was impossible for that friend to be tolerably happy in the lot she had chosen.

How does Austen present Elizabeth and Charlotte's differing attitudes to marriage in this extract, and in the novel as a whole?

2) How does Jane Austen make you feel differently about the character of Mr Darcy in two different chapters of the novel?

3) How does Jane Austen present Mrs Bennet's relationship with her daughters in the novel?

4) Referring to the relationship between Elizabeth and Mr Darcy and between Jane and Mr Bingley, explain how Jane Austen shows how differences in social class have an influence on marriage.

Character Profile — Elizabeth Bennet

Oh good, it's Lizzy — she's my favourite character. Not very original I know.

Elizabeth is the romantic heroine

1) Elizabeth is the <u>main character</u> in the novel — the story is told mostly from <u>her point of view</u>.

© Everett Collection/Rex Features

2) The novel focuses on her <u>changing relationship</u> with Darcy and how Elizabeth's character also <u>changes</u> and <u>grows</u>.

3) Elizabeth is <u>playful</u> and <u>lively</u>, which was <u>unusual</u> at the time — women were <u>expected</u> to be quiet and <u>gentle</u>. <u>Austen</u> uses the character to express <u>her views</u> of what a woman <u>should</u> be like.

Elizabeth is...

Clever: "Lizzy has something more of quickness than her sisters."

Playful: "she had a lively, playful disposition".

Opinionated: "you give your opinion very decidedly".

Writer's Techniques — Language

Elizabeth often expresses her opinion <u>playfully</u> — she <u>teasingly</u> challenges Darcy to "<u>despise</u> me if you dare". But she can be <u>straightforward</u> too, e.g. she turns down Mr Collins's proposal by telling him, "You could <u>not</u> make *me* happy".

She doesn't always follow social rules

1) Elizabeth follows the social rules <u>enough</u> that she never seems bad-mannered, e.g. she's <u>polite</u> to Mr Collins and Darcy even though she doesn't <u>like</u> them.

2) However, she <u>ignores</u> pointless bits of "decorum" if they stop her doing something important, e.g. she <u>walks</u> to Netherfield <u>alone</u> because she's too <u>worried</u> about Jane to wait for the carriage.

3) Austen <u>contrasts</u> Elizabeth's behaviour with <u>others</u> to show that her behaviour is <u>better</u> than theirs. For example, Miss Bingley thinks she's socially superior to Elizabeth, and often subtly <u>insults</u> her, but Elizabeth stays <u>calm</u> and <u>polite</u>, because she has <u>better</u> manners.

Elizabeth shows both pride and prejudice

By giving Elizabeth flaws, Austen makes her more interesting and realistic.

1) Elizabeth is "<u>determined</u> to hate" Darcy before she really knows him.

2) She <u>stubbornly</u> ignores anyone who defends Darcy, and she <u>immediately</u> accepts Wickham's story about him.

3) Prejudice makes her <u>blind</u> to all of Darcy's <u>good</u> points, and all of Wickham's <u>suspicious</u> behaviour.

Writer's Techniques — Irony

One of the first things that attracts Darcy to Elizabeth is her "fine <u>eyes</u>". This is <u>ironic</u>, because she's <u>blinded</u> by her prejudices against him.

4) Her initial prejudice is caused by Darcy <u>wounding</u> her <u>pride</u> by refusing to dance with her at the first ball.

5) She thinks she's a <u>good judge</u> of character — "I... have prided myself on my discernment" — so she stubbornly <u>sticks</u> to her original opinion of Darcy and Wickham.

6) Although Elizabeth has <u>flaws</u>, she <u>grows</u> and <u>changes</u> during the novel. She eventually <u>recognises</u> that her own <u>pride</u> and <u>prejudice</u> have been a <u>barrier</u> to her happiness with Darcy.

Character Profile — Elizabeth Bennet

Elizabeth and Darcy's debates reveal a lot about their relationship, so pay attention and don't skim over them.

Elizabeth's conversations with Darcy show her best features

1) Even though Elizabeth <u>dislikes</u> Darcy, their conversations together bring out the <u>best</u> of her <u>intelligence</u> and <u>wit</u>. This is an early sign to the reader that Elizabeth and Darcy are <u>ideally suited</u>.

2) She's determined to <u>disagree</u> with him, but instead of insulting him she makes <u>intelligent points</u> about the flaws in his opinions. E.g. When he talks about Charlotte living an "easy distance" from her family, Elizabeth points out that distance is "relative".

3) She's also <u>playful</u>, and <u>teases</u> Darcy, for example saying she's "convinced" that he "has no defect".

4) However, Elizabeth's teasing never seems <u>cruel</u>. E.g. When Bingley calls Darcy "awful", Elizabeth sees that he is "<u>offended</u>" and doesn't laugh.

5) <u>Darcy's letter</u> in Chapter 35 shows Elizabeth how <u>prejudiced</u> she's been — she calls herself "blind, partial, prejudiced, absurd." Her reaction shows that she's <u>honest</u> enough to admit that she was wrong, and <u>brave</u> enough to <u>confront</u> her <u>flaws</u>.

Theme — Pride and Prejudice
Elizabeth's <u>relationship</u> with Darcy shows that she's <u>willing</u> to <u>change</u> her opinions. Austen uses this to show how she <u>develops</u> as a character.

Austen uses Elizabeth to show that women can be strong-willed

1) Austen portrays Elizabeth as <u>strong-minded</u> — she makes <u>hard choices</u> to stay <u>true</u> to her <u>beliefs</u>. For example, she turns down <u>two proposals</u>, even though marriage would give her <u>financial security</u>, because she believes that <u>love</u> is more important than "worldly advantage."

2) Elizabeth <u>stands up</u> for herself. When Lady Catherine tries to <u>bully</u> her she replies to all of Lady Catherine's insults <u>calmly and reasonably</u>, but she <u>refuses</u> to just do as she's told.

3) Austen uses a lot of <u>contrasts</u> and <u>parallels</u> to present Elizabeth's personality as the <u>perfect mix</u>:

• She's <u>bold</u> and <u>independent</u> — but unlike Lydia she never takes it <u>too far</u>.
• She's <u>kind</u> and polite — but she's not a <u>pushover</u> like <u>Jane</u>.
• She enjoys <u>mocking</u> people — but, unlike <u>Mr Bennet</u>, she knows that some things are <u>serious</u>.

4) In the end, Elizabeth marries a man she loves and respects. This <u>supports</u> Austen's message that women should act as they believe is <u>right</u>, rather than as society <u>expects</u> them to.

Theme — Marriage
In a society where women often had to marry <u>well</u> for financial <u>security</u>, Elizabeth <u>turns down</u> Mr Collins <u>and</u> Darcy — she's determined to marry for <u>love</u>.

 KEY QUOTE *"Till this moment I never knew myself."*
The nice thing about Elizabeth is that she gets to know herself better as time goes by. She recognises her own flaws and realises that she's been a) too proud and b) too prejudiced. I sense a title brewing...

Character Profile — The Bennet Sisters

Imagine having five daughters to cope with. No wonder the Bennets dropped the ball a bit with the last one.

Jane is kind, but too willing to believe the best of people

1) Jane's <u>kind</u> and <u>beautiful</u>. Elizabeth teases her that she thinks the <u>best</u> of everyone — she takes "the good of everybody's character and make it still <u>better</u>". She's "mild and steady", not witty or lively like Elizabeth.

2) Jane provides a <u>cautious</u> attitude that <u>contrasts</u> with Elizabeth's quickness to <u>form opinions</u>. E.g. Instead of believing Wickham's rumours about Darcy, Jane "urged the possibility of mistakes".

> **Jane is...**
>
> **Kind:** "To have his errors made public might ruin him for ever... We must not make him desperate."
>
> **Forgiving:** "We must endeavour to forget all that has passed".

3) Jane's behaviour suggests that <u>caution</u> can be a <u>good thing</u>, but too much of it can cause <u>problems</u>. Jane's caution means she <u>doesn't</u> make shallow judgements — but she nearly <u>loses</u> Bingley because she's too cautious to show her <u>true feelings</u>.

Lydia is wild and gets into trouble

The Bennet sisters each represent one or two characteristics — they aren't developed into realistic, complex characters. This makes Elizabeth's rounded personality stand out.

1) Lydia is even more <u>lively</u> than Elizabeth, with "<u>high animal spirits</u>". The contrast between them shows that Elizabeth's liveliness is intelligent and polite, but Lydia's is <u>silly</u> and often <u>rude</u>.

2) Her <u>wild</u> behaviour is due to "<u>neglect</u> and <u>mistaken indulgence</u>" — so she also shows the flaws of Mr and Mrs Bennet as irresponsible parents.

3) Lydia's behaviour is an important <u>plot device</u>. Her bad manners and inappropriate flirting are an <u>obstacle</u> to her sisters' marriage prospects. They also hint to the reader that she could cause a <u>serious scandal</u> — this creates <u>tension</u> and <u>drama</u> in the novel.

> **Lydia is...**
>
> **Rowdy:** "we talked and laughed so loud, that anybody might have heard us ten miles off!"
>
> **Flirtatious:** "the most determined flirt that ever made herself or her family ridiculous."

Kitty is influenced by Lydia, and Mary is influenced by books

1) <u>Kitty</u> is Lydia's sidekick — she's interested in the same things and Lydia's influence makes her silly and <u>shallow</u>.

2) When Kitty spends more time with Jane and Elizabeth, she <u>improves</u>.

1) <u>Mary's</u> "plain", so she can't compete with her sisters — because of this she spends most of her time <u>studying</u> and <u>practising the piano</u>.

2) She's <u>not clever</u> or <u>talented</u> — her speeches are <u>inappropriate</u> and her music is "<u>affected</u>".

© AF archive / Alamy

KEY QUOTE

"Vain, ignorant, idle, and absolutely uncontrolled!"

It can be absolute chaos in the Bennet household — giddy Lydia and twitty Kitty are completely out of control, and always squealing about officers. No wonder Jane and Elizabeth are keen to get out of there.

Character Profile — Mr and Mrs Bennet

Austen basically uses these two as a comedy duo. Mr Bennet you laugh with, Mrs Bennet you laugh at.

Mr Bennet never takes anything seriously

1) Mr Bennet is likeable — he's <u>clever</u> and has a <u>dry sense of humour</u>.
   For example, he <u>teases</u> Mrs Bennet about her nerves — "I have a high
   respect for your nerves. They are my old friends."

2) His attitude to Mr Collins shows that he <u>enjoys mocking</u> people.
   Mr Bennet has "great <u>hopes</u> of finding him quite the <u>reverse</u>" of sensible.

3) He and Elizabeth often share the <u>same opinion</u> — he takes her <u>side</u>
   about Mr Collins and says "I will <u>never</u> see you again if you <u>do</u>"
   marry him. This makes the reader view him mostly <u>positively</u>.

Mrs Bennet is a very silly woman

A caricature is a character who has a few exaggerated personality traits. Austen uses caricatures for comic effect, but also to criticise certain character flaws.

1) Mrs Bennet isn't very bright and has an "<u>uncertain
   temper</u>." She's a <u>caricature</u> because she's so
   <u>hysterical</u> and unaware of her own flaws.

2) Austen uses her to create <u>ironic humour</u> in the novel — all she cares
   about is getting her daughters <u>married</u>, but her rudeness and ignorance
   make her the biggest <u>obstacle</u> to their marriage prospects.

3) But Austen uses this <u>humour</u> to make a <u>serious</u> point. Mrs Bennet's
   <u>materialism</u> (interest in wealth) and lack of <u>self-awareness</u> set a bad
   example for Lydia and contribute to her <u>recklessness</u>.

They show the danger of a marriage based on shallow attraction

1) Austen uses their relationship to show that physical
   attraction <u>alone</u> is not enough for a <u>happy</u> marriage.
   Their marriage was based on "<u>youth</u> and <u>beauty</u>",
   but they had nothing in common and now there is
   no "<u>real affection</u>" between them.

Theme — Marriage
Austen draws parallels between the <u>Bennets'</u>
marriage and that of <u>Lydia</u> and <u>Wickham</u>,
suggesting that they will end up just as <u>unhappy</u>.

2) The only <u>happiness</u> Mr Bennet gets from the relationship is in <u>laughing</u> at his wife's "<u>ignorance</u>
   and <u>folly</u>", and Mrs Bennet is completely unable to "<u>understand</u> his character".

3) Their <u>unhappy marriage</u> also affects their <u>children</u> negatively. Mrs Bennet is a <u>bad influence</u> who
   encourages Lydia and Kitty to be flirtatious and silly, and Mr Bennet does nothing to <u>stop</u> her.
   He would rather <u>avoid</u> them, or <u>laugh</u> at them, than try to <u>improve</u> them.

4) It's partly because Elizabeth has seen all the "<u>disadvantages</u>" of "so unsuitable a marriage"
   that she is <u>determined</u> to marry someone she <u>loves</u> and <u>respects</u>.

Write about Austen's use of irony...

All Mrs Bennet wants is for her daughters to marry rich men, but she's the one who nearly scares off Bingley
and Darcy. Mr Bennet would enjoy the irony (if he ever paid any attention) — and you can write about it.

Character Profile — Mr Darcy

Fitzwilliam Darcy is the hero, but he's a hero in disguise at first. Disguised as a tall, brooding, handsome man with an impressive fortune, who's irresistibly drawn to the heroine's beautiful eyes... you'd never guess...

Mr Darcy is the romantic hero — eventually...

© Moviestore collection Ltd / Alamy

1) The novel is written from <u>Elizabeth's</u> point of view, not Darcy's, so it's <u>not</u> immediately clear that he's the hero — he's just a man who was rude to her at a ball.

2) Austen makes him an <u>interesting</u>, realistic character with <u>flaws</u>. These flaws mean that Elizabeth initially <u>dislikes</u> him.

3) His <u>good points</u> are gradually developed as the novel progresses, but his role as Elizabeth's <u>true love</u> isn't revealed until <u>later</u> on.

Mr Darcy is...

Proud: "Could you expect me to... congratulate myself on the hope of relations, whose condition in life is so decidedly beneath my own?"

Unforgiving: "my good opinion, once lost, is lost forever."

Generous: "to give his money freely... to assist his tenants, and relieve the poor."

Mr Darcy makes a bad first impression

See p.54 for more on Darcy's language.

1) Austen first introduces Mr Darcy to the reader in a very <u>public setting</u> — a ball at Meryton. This setting presents all of Darcy's <u>worst</u> qualities.

2) His character is shown mainly through the <u>opinions</u> of <u>others</u> — and his actions are <u>interpreted</u> very <u>negatively</u> by the crowd. He <u>dances</u> only twice, and only <u>speaks</u> to people he <u>already</u> knows. Based on these actions, everybody decides Darcy is "<u>forbidding</u>", "above his company" and "<u>disagreeable</u>".

3) He also won't dance with Elizabeth because he refuses to "give consequence to young ladies who are <u>slighted</u> by other men" (she doesn't have a dance partner). This <u>suggests</u> that he is rude and <u>arrogant</u>.

Austen drops hints that he's nice really

Austen develops Darcy as a complex, realistic character — and keeps the reader guessing about what he's really like.

1) When we see Darcy in the <u>private</u> setting of Netherfield, the more <u>likeable</u> side of his <u>personality</u> emerges:

- Darcy is <u>attracted</u> to Elizabeth for all the <u>right</u> reasons — not just her looks. He thinks her expression is "uncommonly <u>intelligent</u>" and he's drawn to her <u>kindness</u> and <u>liveliness</u>.

- He isn't affected by <u>Miss Bingley's</u> flattery — he listens to her with "<u>indifference</u>" and doesn't let her compliments <u>go to his head</u>. He's not as <u>arrogant</u> as he seems.

- He seems to have strong morals. For example, he says "whatever bears affinity to <u>cunning</u> is despicable", which suggests he doesn't like people who are sly or dishonest.

2) But his <u>snobbish attitude</u> is also developed. He thinks country society is "<u>confined</u> and unvarying" and doesn't <u>want</u> to be attracted to Elizabeth because of "the <u>inferiority</u> of her <u>connections</u>".

Character Profile — Mr Darcy

Darcy, Darcy, give me an answer dooo. I'm half crazy, having to analyse you. It won't be a golden essay — in fact it's rather messy. You're very proud, and too high-browed, but Elizabeth still loves yoouu.

Darcy is complex and mysterious

1) Austen gives a lot of <u>evidence</u> that Elizabeth is right to <u>dislike</u> Darcy:

- He's proud, but says this isn't a flaw because his "<u>superiority</u> of mind" keeps it "under good regulation".
- Wickham's story makes Darcy seem <u>cruel</u>, <u>vindictive</u> and <u>dishonest</u>.
- Colonel Fitzwilliam's description of how Darcy <u>split up</u> Bingley and Jane also makes him seem <u>cruel</u> and proves that he's <u>prejudiced</u> against people because of their <u>family connections</u>.

2) But his <u>immoral</u> behaviour is only described through <u>rumours</u> — the behaviour the reader <u>sees</u> is <u>respectable</u>, honourable, and sometimes <u>kind</u>.

3) The wordplay and <u>flirtation</u> between him and Elizabeth suggests that Darcy is a <u>possible</u> love interest — this creates <u>suspense</u> as the reader wonders if Darcy's role is <u>hero</u> or <u>villain</u>.

Elizabeth challenges Darcy's pride and prejudices

1) Darcy's main <u>flaws</u> are <u>pride</u> in his social status and <u>prejudice</u> against people who are socially 'inferior'. These flaws are <u>obstacles</u> to his <u>relationship</u> with Elizabeth — he has to <u>overcome</u> them before they can be united.

2) Darcy's <u>first</u> proposal is important for his <u>development</u> as a character. Elizabeth's criticisms of his "<u>arrogance</u>... <u>conceit</u>, and... <u>selfish disdain</u>" make him start to <u>realise</u> that his proud, snobby manners and social prejudice are "unpardonable".

Theme — Social Class

Austen uses Darcy to <u>criticise</u> the way <u>upper</u> classes look down on the <u>lower</u> classes. As Darcy loses his class prejudices, he <u>opens up</u> to new relationships with Elizabeth and the Gardiners that make him a much <u>happier</u> and more <u>likeable</u> character.

© WORKING TITLE / THE KOBAL COLLECTION

3) The next time Elizabeth sees Darcy, at Pemberley, his manners are "<u>polite</u>, and <u>unassuming</u>" and he makes an effort to get to know the Gardiners, who are socially '<u>beneath</u>' him. This shows that Darcy has managed to <u>overcome</u> his social prejudice.

4) The most <u>dramatic evidence</u> of Darcy's changing character is his behaviour during the <u>Wickham scandal</u>. Paying off Wickham demonstrates that he is willing to <u>swallow</u> his <u>pride</u> to prove his <u>love</u>.

5) By the end of the novel, Darcy has learnt to judge people on their <u>personal merits</u>. For example, he "really loved" the Gardiners, despite their <u>lower social class</u>.

Mention that Elizabeth's viewpoint is biased...

Pride and Prejudice has an omniscient narrator (have a look at p.56), but it follows Elizabeth's perspective pretty closely. It's only when we get other views on Darcy that we start to realise he's actually a nice guy.

Character Profile — Mr Bingley and his Sisters

Bingley's a lot like his true love, Jane — all sweetness and light. His sisters, on the other hand...

Bingley is a strong contrast to Darcy

1) Unlike Darcy, Bingley:

- Makes a good first impression — everyone's delighted with his friendliness and "unaffected" manners".

- Isn't snobby or prejudiced. When his sisters are laughing at the Bennet family, he says that "If they had uncles enough to fill *all* Cheapside... it would not make them one jot less agreeable."

Bingley is handsome, rich and kind — and too good to be realistic. He represents the ideal traits of a husband, but his character's not developed enough to be convincing or lifelike.

2) However, there's no mystery with Bingley — he's completely open about his feelings. Like Jane, Mr Bingley doesn't have any major flaws, so he doesn't change during the novel.

3) Bingley is modest and trusting, which makes him likeable but a bit weak. He believes Darcy's claim that Jane doesn't love him, instead of sticking to his own opinion and fighting for the woman he loves.

Mr Bingley is...

Kind: "giving his housekeeper directions that every possible attention might be paid to the sick lady".

Enthusiastic: "Bingley had never met with more pleasant people or prettier girls in his life".

Bingley's sisters are snobbish and superficial

1) Mrs Louisa Hurst and Miss Caroline Bingley are "conceited" and very class-conscious (snobby).

2) Austen uses the Bingley sisters to reveal the hypocrisy of class prejudices:

- Their father made his fortune "by trade" (through business). This makes it ironic that they look down on the Bennet sisters for their middle-class relations.

- They show the superficial aspects of the upper classes. They're "very fine ladies" — educated and fashionable — but they're unkind and two-faced. For example, they do their best to separate their brother from their "dear friend" Jane, even though it'll make Bingley and Jane unhappy.

3) Miss Bingley tries to flirt with Darcy, which creates some comic scenes, as her flattery is ridiculous.

4) She provides a contrast to Elizabeth, who talks to Darcy as an equal and challenges him. Ironically, it's Miss Bingley's criticisms of Elizabeth that make Darcy admit how much he likes her.

"He is just what a young man ought to be"

Bingley's warm, open nature pretty much makes him the anti-Darcy — right from the beginning of the novel, he's presented as quite a catch for any young woman in the market for a man. Jane's a lucky lady.

Character Profile — Mr Wickham

Aha, it's Wickham at last — I do love a dastardly scoundrel.

At first, Wickham seems to be the romantic hero of the novel

1) The structure of a traditional romance novel begins with the hero and heroine falling in love, then overcoming numerous obstacles before reaching the happy ending when they can finally be together.

2) When Wickham first appears, he's presented as a romantic hero — handsome, with "a fine countenance" (face) and friendly, with a "happy readiness of conversation". Wickham and Elizabeth's mutual attraction makes the reader believe that he may be the main love interest of the novel.

3) He also seems to be brave in the face of terrible unkindness. The story he tells Elizabeth about Darcy cheating him out of his inheritance makes Wickham seem completely innocent. He also says he will never "defy or expose" Darcy, because he was very fond of Darcy's father and wants to respect his memory. This makes him seem honourable.

4) Supposedly, Darcy is the reason Wickham has no financial security — so Darcy's cruelty seems like the obstacle the lovers have to overcome.

Writer's Techniques — Language

Wickham often sounds emotional and a bit over the top — he says he's "grieved to the soul by a thousand tender recollections" of Darcy's father. He also contradicts himself, for example he says he will not "expose" Darcy, but he describes Darcy's "scandalous" behaviour.

Mr Wickham is...

Charming: "he is... the most agreeable man I ever saw".

Mercenary: "Mr Wickham's chief object was unquestionably my sister's fortune".

Dishonest: "he has neither integrity nor honour."

But he turns out to be a villain

1) Wickham's behaviour towards Miss King suggests that he's not completely honourable. He "paid her not the smallest attention" until she inherited the money, so he seems "mercenary" (greedy).

2) Darcy's letter reveals that Wickham's a liar who seduced Georgiana to get her fortune. This shows Elizabeth his real character.

3) The scandal of Lydia and Wickham's elopement threatens to keep Elizabeth and Darcy apart just when they begin to grow close.

4) Now, Wickham's role has flipped from poor but honourable victim to immoral villain whose lies kept Darcy and Elizabeth apart. This dramatic change creates a lot of excitement in the novel.

Writer's Techniques — Irony

- It's ironic that Wickham seemed to be the hero — actually his lies are a major obstacle to Darcy and Elizabeth's relationship.
- It's also ironic that Wickham's behaviour forces Darcy to overcome his pride — which proves Darcy's love for Elizabeth.

Theme — Love

When Elizabeth hears Darcy's story, she sees that her attraction to Wickham was based on his looks and charm. This emphasises the message that first appearances are often wrong.

© Moviestore collection Ltd / Alamy

 KEY QUOTE **"He smiled, looked handsome, and said many pretty things."**
Even after the Bennets know Wickham's true colours, he still puts on a show when he visits them, trying to charm them all. Elizabeth thinks she was "blind" about him, but he's very good at putting on an act.

Character Profile — Mr Collins and the Lucas Family

Moving swiftly on, from scoundrels to, erm, idiots.

Mr Collins is a pompous snob

1) Mr Collins is a comedy character. Elizabeth and her father enjoy laughing at his "pompous" and "narrow-minded" attitude. His attempts to make a good impression by constantly complimenting everyone he meets are clearly ridiculous.

See p.55 for more on satire.

Writer's Techniques — Satire

- In Austen's day, some landowners could choose their own vicar. This meant that vicars weren't always chosen for their moral or religious views, and some were completely unsuitable for the role.

- Austen uses Mr Collins to satirise this practice. His attitude is very unchristian — he's materialistic, snobby and unforgiving.

Writer's Techniques — Language

Mr Collins only says what he thinks other people want to hear, which makes him sound fake and sycophantic, e.g. he admits to spending time thinking up "little elegant compliments". He often repeats the same ideas, e.g. "to follow the dictates of my conscience... to perform what I look on as a point of duty". This makes him sound boring and unintelligent.

2) Austen uses him to satirise people who put too much importance on social status. He doesn't see Lady Catherine's rudeness and snobbery, but thinks she's wonderful just because she's a rich aristocrat.

Charlotte Lucas marries Mr Collins for financial security

Copyright © BBC Photo Library

1) Charlotte acts as a contrast to Elizabeth by representing the unromantic reasons for marriage. Her decisions also reveal the social pressure placed on women to get married.

2) Charlotte views marriage as "the only provision for well-educated young women of small fortune". Mr Collins can give her a comfortable life, so she doesn't care that he's annoying.

3) Elizabeth is disappointed and upset that Charlotte can marry for purely practical reasons — she thinks it will be "impossible" for Charlotte to be even "tolerably happy".

4) Austen's opinion of the marriage is less clear-cut. It's left to the reader to decide if Charlotte's "evident enjoyment" in her house is worth the burden of having a husband she avoids "as much as possible".

Charlotte's family aren't as sensible as she is

1) Austen uses Charlotte's family to reinforce her message about the snobbery of Regency society.

2) Sir William Lucas was a businessman, but he was given a knighthood, and now he thinks he has to act like gentry. He and his daughter Maria are overwhelmed by Lady Catherine. Her social status affects their judgement so they don't realise how rude she is. This shows their prejudices about class and wealth.

KEY QUOTE

"I am not romantic, you know; I never was."

Mr Collins isn't exactly a catch, but Charlotte's family aren't rich enough to do better, and she doesn't want to be a burden. Her marriage is a practical one, which contrasts with lots of other marriages in the novel.

Section Three — Characters

Character Profile — Lady Catherine and Anne

What a disappointment these two are, after all Mr Collins's high praise.

Lady Catherine is rude and bossy

1) Austen presents Lady Catherine as a humorous <u>caricature</u> rather than a <u>realistic personality</u> and uses her to <u>satirise</u> the outdated attitudes and snobbery of the aristocracy.

2) Her <u>pride</u> in her own <u>status</u> makes her behave <u>rudely</u>, e.g. she makes her guests <u>uncomfortable</u> with "the impertinence of her questions".

Writer's Techniques — Language

Lady Catherine is <u>openly critical</u> — she tells Elizabeth she will "never play really <u>well</u>" at the piano, even though Lady Catherine can't play <u>at all</u>. She <u>arrogantly assumes</u> "If I had ever learnt, I should have been a <u>great</u> proficient."

Lady Catherine is...

Interfering: "she sallied forth... to settle their differences, silence their complaints, and scold them".

Rude: "I will not be interrupted. Hear me in silence."

Snobby: "She likes to have the distinction of rank preserved."

3) She <u>encourages</u> the "<u>excessive admiration</u>" of Mr Collins — this shows that she's a <u>snob</u> who believes in keeping people in their place.

4) She's also <u>obsessed</u> with preserving her <u>bloodline</u>, so she <u>insists</u> Darcy and her daughter are "<u>destined</u> for each other" simply because they're related.

She shows that a higher status doesn't make you a better person

1) Darcy's family connections are <u>superior</u> to Elizabeth's <u>embarrassing</u> relatives, but Lady Catherine and Mrs Bennet actually show some <u>similarities</u>, even though they have different <u>backgrounds</u>.

2) Austen draws <u>parallels</u> in their <u>behaviour</u> to show that bad manners aren't linked to social class. E.g.

- Mrs Bennet <u>embarrasses</u> Elizabeth: she "blushed and blushed again with <u>shame</u> and vexation".
- But Lady Catherine also <u>embarrasses</u> Darcy: he "looked a little <u>ashamed</u> of his aunt's ill-breeding".

© AF archive / Alamy

Anne de Bourgh is quiet and dull

1) Miss de Bourgh only has a <u>small role</u> in the novel. She's another <u>rival</u> for Mr Darcy's affection, but the only thing going for her is the fact that their marriage would "<u>unite the two estates</u>".

2) She's portrayed as fairly <u>pathetic</u> — Maria Lucas is amazed that she's such "a <u>little</u> creature... so thin and small". Austen uses her to <u>mock</u> the belief that noble bloodlines need to be <u>preserved</u> — an ancient heritage doesn't automatically produce <u>healthy</u>, <u>clever</u>, or <u>talented</u> people.

Write about how Austen presents the aristocracy...

Austen creates lots of interesting contrasts between the de Bourghs and other characters — for example, between Lady Catherine's and Elizabeth's manners, and the attractions of Elizabeth compared to Anne.

Character Profile — The Gardiners and Mrs Philips

Here are some more of Elizabeth's extended relatives — some very nice, others embarrassing.

The Gardiners are supportive and intelligent

1) Mr and Mrs Gardiner provide a strong <u>contrast</u> with Mr and Mrs Bennet to emphasise the Bennets' <u>flaws</u> as <u>parents</u>.

2) Mr and Mrs Gardiner provide <u>comfort</u> and <u>support</u> for the Bennet girls when they <u>need</u> it.

3) For example, when <u>Jane's upset</u> about Bingley they invite her to <u>stay</u> with them to try and <u>take her mind off it</u>. In contrast, Mr Bennet <u>jokes</u> that girls enjoy being "crossed in love", and Mrs Bennet won't <u>stop talking</u> about the <u>disappointment</u>.

4) Mrs Gardiner gives <u>sensible</u> advice. For example, she's sure Darcy is <u>in love</u> with Elizabeth. She tells her niece that "he wants nothing but a little more liveliness, and *that*... his <u>wife</u> may teach him."

Copyright © BBC Photo Library

5) Mr Gardiner is <u>clever</u> and <u>capable</u>. During the scandal with Lydia he goes to London to <u>help</u>, writes letters to keep the family <u>informed</u>, and promises them that they can "depend on my <u>diligence</u> and <u>care</u>".

Austen uses the Gardiners to criticise class prejudice

1) The Gardiners are kind and sensible. Mr Gardiner is "<u>gentlemanlike</u>" and <u>well-educated</u>. Mrs Gardiner is "amiable" and "intelligent".

2) However, Mr Gardiner is a <u>businessman</u> who lives "within view of his own warehouses" in London. He's <u>middle class</u> and works for a living — which is why some characters <u>look down</u> on him.

3) Austen uses the Gardiners to show how <u>wrong</u> class prejudices are. It's obvious that the Gardiners are really <u>nice</u> people — but people like Miss Bingley <u>judge</u> them simply because of their <u>social status</u>.

Theme — Prejudice

The Gardiners help Darcy to <u>overcome</u> his class <u>prejudice</u> — when he first meets them, Elizabeth "glories" in all the <u>intelligent</u> things they say and by the end of the novel he "really <u>loved</u>" them.

Mrs Philips is Mrs Bennet's sister

1) Mrs Philips is <u>similar</u> to her sister — <u>very silly</u>. She's also "<u>vulgar</u>" (rude and with bad manners).

2) She reinforces the impression that most of Elizabeth's family is <u>embarrassing</u> and inappropriate. After Elizabeth gets engaged she does her best to "<u>shield</u>" Darcy from having to talk to her aunt.

"*Mr. Gardiner was a sensible, gentlemanlike man*"

Mrs Philips and Mrs Bennet are two peas in a pod, but the Gardiners are a different kettle of fish entirely. Right, enough food analogies — remember to write about what the Gardiners suggest about class prejudice.

Character Profile — Other Characters

Here are two more characters worth knowing about. They don't have very big roles, but they're still important.

Georgiana reveals Darcy's softer side

1) Georgiana and Darcy are very <u>close</u> — he often <u>writes</u> to her and speaks about her with "affectionate praise".

2) At first she's only described through other characters' <u>opinions</u> of her, so the reader isn't sure what to believe — Miss Bingley says she "<u>delighted</u> me" but Wickham says Georgiana is "<u>proud</u>".

3) When Elizabeth finally meets her, she sees that Georgiana has a lot of <u>positive</u> character traits — she has "<u>sense</u>", "<u>good humour</u>" and is very "accomplished" (she plays the piano, draws and dances). Her pride is just <u>shyness</u>.

4) Georgiana is a lot <u>younger</u> and more <u>timid</u> than Darcy. She's also female — which means she's less <u>independent</u> than he is.

Copyright © BBC Photo Library

Theme — Social Class

Georgiana <u>almost</u> eloped with Wickham, nearly making the <u>same mistake</u> as Lydia. This reinforces Austen's message that <u>social class</u> doesn't necessarily make a <u>difference</u> to how people <u>behave</u>. It also explains why Darcy is <u>sympathetic</u> about Lydia's scandal.

5) Austen uses Georgiana to represent Darcy's <u>emotional vulnerability</u>. She shows his <u>kindness</u> and capacity for <u>love</u>, but she's also his <u>weak spot</u>. This is emphasised by the story of Wickham's <u>seduction</u> of Georgiana — which was motivated partly by his desire to get <u>revenge</u> on Darcy.

Colonel Fitzwilliam is charming but practical

Look at pages 44-45 for more about marriage.

1) Through the character of Colonel Fitzwilliam, Austen develops the theme of marrying for <u>financial stability</u>. Elizabeth "<u>caught his fancy</u> very much" but he tells her <u>plainly</u> that he's going to have to <u>marry</u> with "some attention to <u>money</u>", because his older brother will inherit most of the family money.

Theme — Marriage

Colonel Fitzwilliam is another example of a <u>good</u> character who needs to marry for <u>money</u> instead of <u>love</u>. His situation shows that <u>inheritance issues</u> affected <u>men</u> as well as <u>women</u>.

2) Austen also uses him to create another <u>obstacle</u> for Darcy and Elizabeth to overcome, as he <u>accidentally</u> reveals to Elizabeth that Darcy split up Bingley and Jane. This <u>infuriates</u> Elizabeth and makes her <u>dislike</u> Darcy <u>even more</u>.

3) However, he is <u>also</u> one of the reasons Elizabeth begins to <u>trust</u> Darcy and re-examine her <u>prejudices</u> against him. Darcy says that "the truth of everything" in his letter can be <u>confirmed</u> by Colonel Fitzwilliam. Elizabeth <u>trusts</u> and <u>likes</u> Colonel Fitzwilliam, and realises that Darcy is telling the <u>truth</u>.

EXAM TIP

Don't forget about the minor characters...

There are loads of characters in the novel, and even the ones who don't appear very much (like Colonel Fitzwilliam and Georgiana) are important. Make sure you're confident writing about every character.

Practice Questions

OK, it's question time again — you're going to find out how well you really know these characters.

Quick Questions

1) Which of the five Bennet girls is each of the following statements describing?
   a) Easily-led, silly and fretful
   b) Sweet, kind and gentle
   c) Bookish and keen to seem "accomplished"
   d) Bright, witty and playful
   e) High-spirited, thoughtless and wild.

2) Describe in two sentences how Darcy seems to change throughout the book.

3) Write down two qualities Bingley has that make him instantly popular with others.

4) Give one of Wickham's qualities that is attractive, and one that is unpleasant.

5) Choose four words that sum up the character of Mr Collins.

In-depth Questions

1) Elizabeth Bennet claims she has always "prided" herself on her "discernment", which means the ability to judge wisely. Do you think she's right to do this? Explain your answer.

2) Read the following quote from Mr Bennet, describing how he feels after Lydia runs away:
"...let me once in my life feel how much I have been to blame. I am not afraid of being overpowered by the impression. It will pass away soon enough."

What does this tell you about the character of Mr Bennet?

3) Look at the following statement:
"Mr Darcy is misjudged by others throughout much of *Pride and Prejudice*, but this is at least partially his own fault."

Explain whether you agree or disagree with this statement and why.

4) How does Austen show the reader that Miss Bingley is:
   a) jealous
   b) a snob.

5) Lady Catherine is the only aristocratic person (i.e. with inherited wealth and a title) in the novel. What do you think Lady Catherine's character tells you about Austen's opinion of titles and money?

Practice Questions

If you whizzed through those first questions, you'll be glad to get your teeth into something a bit more challenging. This little lot have got a real exam-style flavour to them. Delicious.

Exam-style Questions

1) Use this extract to answer the questions that follow.

> "If your master would marry, you might see more of him."
>
> "Yes, Sir; but I do not know when *that* will be. I do not know who is good enough for him."
>
> Mr. and Mrs. Gardiner smiled. Elizabeth could not help saying, "It is very much to his credit, I am sure, that you should think so."
>
> "I say no more than the truth, and what everybody will say that knows him," replied the other. Elizabeth thought this was going pretty far; and she listened with increasing astonishment as the housekeeper added, "I have never had a cross word from him in my life, and I have known him ever since he was four years old."
>
> This was praise, of all others most extraordinary, most opposite to her ideas. That he was not a good-tempered man had been her firmest opinion. Her keenest attention was awakened; she longed to hear more, and was grateful to her uncle for saying:
>
> "There are very few people of whom so much can be said. You are lucky in having such a master."
>
> "Yes, Sir, I know I am. If I was to go through the world, I could not meet with a better. But I have always observed that they who are good-natured when children, are good-natured when they grow up; and he was always the sweetest-tempered, most generous-hearted boy in the world."
>
> Elizabeth almost stared at her. "Can this be Mr. Darcy?" thought she.

Answer all of the following questions:

a) How does Jane Austen present the character of Mr Darcy here?
   How does it affect the reader's opinion of him?

b) How does Austen present Darcy's changing character in *Pride and Prejudice*?

2) Explain how Elizabeth Bennet displays elements of both pride and prejudice at different points in the novel.

3) How does Jane Austen use language to show the reader the different personalities of Mr Collins and Lady Catherine?

4) How does Austen make the reader feel differently about the character of Wickham in two different chapters of the novel?

Love

Love is one of most important themes of *Pride and Prejudice* — the happiest matches show what Austen felt was important — not social status or shallow attraction, but real understanding and affection.

Relationships that aren't based on love don't work

1) A key <u>message</u> of *Pride and Prejudice* is that relationships should be based on <u>love</u>, not <u>shallow attraction</u>.

2) The <u>unhappy</u> relationships in the novel come about because the characters acted on their <u>first impressions</u>, instead of getting to <u>know</u> their partner properly:

Austen originally called her
novel "First Impressions".

- Mr Bennet was "captivated by <u>youth</u> and <u>beauty</u>" when he married Mrs Bennet, but Mrs Bennet's stupidity soon "put an <u>end</u> to all <u>real affection</u>".

- Lydia and Wickham's relationship is <u>only</u> based on <u>shallow qualities</u> — "their passions were stronger than their virtue". Their affection soon turns to "<u>indifference</u>". This <u>mirrors</u> the Bennets' marriage, and suggests that Lydia and Wickham's marriage will turn out the same way.

3) In contrast, <u>Elizabeth</u> initially <u>dislikes</u> Darcy, and he's not <u>interested</u> in her. Unlike Lydia and Wickham, Darcy and Elizabeth are <u>sensible</u> enough to realise when they've made a <u>mistake</u> and change their <u>opinions</u>. So over time, their first impressions change to <u>true love</u>.

True love is based on gradual understanding

1) Elizabeth and Darcy have to overcome their <u>bad first impressions</u> before their love can succeed.

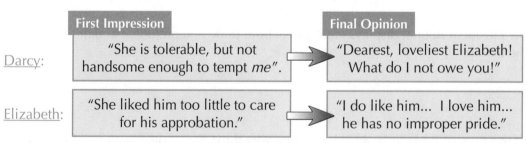

	First Impression		Final Opinion
Darcy:	"She is tolerable, but not handsome enough to tempt *me*".	→	"Dearest, loveliest Elizabeth! What do I not owe you!"
Elizabeth:	"She liked him too little to care for his approbation."	→	"I do like him... I love him... he has no improper pride."

2) They <u>learn</u> from one another and <u>change for the better</u> over the course of the book. Darcy overcomes his <u>pride</u> and Elizabeth her <u>prejudices</u> against him.

3) As Elizabeth and Darcy overcome these obstacles, they become <u>more aware</u> of their own <u>faults</u>, so they also become more <u>tolerant</u> and <u>understanding</u>. This makes their relationship even <u>stronger</u>.

4) They have a <u>balanced relationship</u> which works because of their <u>differences</u>.

5) Unlike Darcy and Elizabeth, <u>Bingley</u> and <u>Jane</u> like each other <u>straight away</u>. But instead of acting on <u>first impressions</u>, they <u>wait</u> to see if the mutual attraction develops into something more. When they finally marry, they <u>know</u> that their relationship is based on <u>true love</u> and real <u>understanding</u>.

Love

What is love? Is it all you need? How deep is it? And can you feel it tonight? I can't answer any of these questions, but I can tell you that it's a pretty important theme in the novel, so here's another page on it.

Austen explores whether love should be private

Austen uses the way different characters <u>behave</u> when they're in <u>love</u> to <u>develop</u> their personalities — some characters try to keep their love <u>private</u>, but others show their feelings <u>openly</u>. For example:

- <u>Jane's</u> feelings are very <u>private</u>. Charlotte says Jane should "show *more* affection" to make Bingley fall in love. Darcy thinks she's not interested in Bingley, so he <u>splits</u> them up.
- Her behaviour shows that she's <u>genuine</u> — she's not going to act <u>falsely</u> or <u>change</u> her personality just to attract a rich husband.

- <u>Miss Bingley's</u> feelings are very <u>public</u>. She flirts with Mr Darcy all the time, even though he's <u>clearly</u> not interested.
- This makes her seem a bit <u>desperate</u>, and her <u>flattery</u> of Darcy shows that she's <u>fake</u>.

Contrasting Jane — a likeable character — with Miss Bingley hints that Austen thinks keeping your feelings private is the better approach.

Women in Regency Society

Charlotte and Jane's different attitudes towards flirting show the <u>conflict</u> women faced at the time — they needed to <u>attract</u> a husband, but they didn't want to appear too <u>forward</u> or <u>desperate</u> as that would damage their <u>reputation</u>.

Characters who listen to both their heart and head are happiest

1) Elizabeth and Darcy's <u>actions</u> show that they both want a relationship that's <u>romantic</u> and <u>sensible</u>:

- Darcy tries to <u>ignore</u> his romantic <u>feelings</u> for Elizabeth because he knows it's not <u>sensible</u> to marry someone whose <u>social status</u> is lower than his own.
- But he also chooses <u>not</u> to marry Anne de Bourgh — it would improve his <u>status</u>, but he doesn't <u>love</u> her.

- Elizabeth realises it wouldn't be <u>sensible</u> to marry Wickham because he's <u>poor</u>.
- But she also <u>refuses</u> to marry Darcy, even though he's very <u>rich</u>, because she thinks she could never <u>love</u> him.

2) In the end their relationship is the <u>happiest</u>, because they <u>resolve</u> the conflict between <u>practicality</u> and <u>romance</u>. Darcy realises that rejecting someone because of their social class is <u>prejudiced</u> rather than <u>practical</u>, and Elizabeth sees that Darcy is "exactly the man who... would most suit her."

3) <u>Unhappy</u> relationships in the novel are controlled too strongly either by the heart or the head:

- <u>Lydia</u> follows her heart — this <u>risks</u> her reputation and results in a <u>loveless</u> marriage.
- <u>Charlotte</u> is too sensible — she marries for <u>financial</u> reasons, but she doesn't <u>like</u> or <u>respect</u> her husband.

KEY QUOTE — *"Perhaps I did not always love him so well as I do now."*

The relationships in the novel show lots of different attitudes to love, and most of the relationships alter over time — the characters get to know each other, so their relationships change. Kind of like real life, really.

Marriage

Marriage is another central theme in *Pride and Prejudice* — it's all some of the characters can think about.

The book starts as it means to go on... with marriage

The importance of the theme of <u>marriage</u> in the book is clear right from the famous <u>opening sentence</u>:

suggests this is the only interpretation   *means that <u>everyone</u> knows this is true*

"It is a truth universally acknowledged, that a single man in
possession of a good fortune, must be in want of a wife."

*stressing what a woman might be looking
for in a possible husband*   *shows the expectation that a man
must want to marry*

1) Austen isn't really being serious here — this opening sentence is <u>ironic</u> (see p.55).

2) She's mocking the way everyone assumes that a young, rich man moving into an area <u>must</u> want to marry one of their daughters. In fact, the <u>opposite</u> is true — in Austen's day, a single <u>woman</u> without a fortune needed a <u>husband</u> (see p.8).

Marriage isn't just about falling in love

1) For many characters, marriage has <u>important benefits</u> — it can improve their lives <u>financially</u> and <u>socially</u>, and give women more <u>freedom</u>.

2) Unmarried women <u>couldn't live alone</u>. Charlotte marries so she can be <u>independent</u> of her family and <u>in control</u> of "her home and her housekeeping".

3) Marrying someone <u>higher up</u> the social ladder could <u>benefit</u> your whole <u>family</u> as well as <u>improving</u> your social status. E.g. Mrs Bennet thinks Jane's engagement will help the <u>other</u> sisters <u>marry well</u> because it'll "<u>throw</u>" them in the way of other <u>rich men</u>".

© WORKING TITLE / THE KOBAL COLLECTION

People married because society expected it

1) There was <u>social pressure</u> to get married — it was <u>expected</u>, even if you didn't really want to. E.g.

- <u>Mr Collins</u> wants to "<u>set the example</u> of matrimony", and Lady Catherine has told him that he "must marry". He's getting married because he thinks he <u>should</u>, but he doesn't mind <u>who</u> he marries.

- It wasn't seen as <u>ladylike</u> for upper-class women to work, so marriage was often the only way a woman could become financially stable. This is why <u>Charlotte</u> marries "without thinking highly... of matrimony".

- <u>Lydia</u> says she'd be "<u>ashamed</u>... of not being married" — it was <u>embarrassing</u> to be an "<u>old maid</u>".

2) None of these characters have <u>happy</u> marriages — Austen is <u>criticising</u> the way that people act how <u>society</u> expects them to, rather than doing what they <u>want</u> to do.

Marriage

Yet more reasons to get married coming up. No pressure or anything...

Money is important when you're deciding who to marry...

1) Elizabeth's attitude towards marrying for money probably reveals Austen's own views about it.

2) Elizabeth thinks marriage should be a balance between practicality and love. She refuses Mr Collins and Mr Darcy because she doesn't love them. However, she accepts that financial reasons are important too — for example she sees it's a bad idea to marry Wickham because of his "want of fortune".

3) Elizabeth expects other characters to show the same balance between practicality and love:

> Elizabeth is shocked and upset when Charlotte Lucas marries Mr Collins purely for the "disinterested desire of an establishment".

> Elizabeth thinks it's unwise to marry someone just because of their wealth, and not care about their personality. Elizabeth judges Charlotte because she ignores Mr Collins' horrible personality and only marries him for his money.

> But Elizabeth doesn't blame Wickham when he starts to court Miss King, because he needs "something to live on" and Miss King is a "good sort".

> Elizabeth thinks it's acceptable to marry someone for their money, as long as they have something in common and a reasonable personality — Elizabeth thinks Wickham is being sensible to try to like Miss King.

...but personality is even more important

1) The most unhappy marriages in the novel are the ones where the couple have nothing in common:

> Mr Bennet likes to "have his library to himself", and often retreats there. He has lost all "real affection" for his wife, and the only pleasure he gets from her company is that "her ignorance and folly... contributed to his amusement."

> Charlotte makes her life comfortable by encouraging Mr Collins to work in the garden "as much as possible", so that he can be "often forgotten". She's "ashamed" of her husband's ridiculous speeches, but ignores them.

2) Mrs Bennet and Mr Collins aren't improved by marriage.

3) This contrasts with Elizabeth and Darcy's happy relationship — Darcy is "softened" by Elizabeth and she benefits from his "judgement, information, and knowledge". They each care enough about the other to want to change, and they're influenced by each other's good qualities.

4) This reinforces Austen's message that personality is the most important factor in a happy marriage.

Discuss Elizabeth's attitude towards marriage...

Show the examiner that you understand what Elizabeth's looking for in a husband. She's not just looking for security — she wants love, too. Pretty brave... as an "old maid" she'd have to keep living with Mr and Mrs B...

Social Class

Social class was everything in Jane Austen's day — it was much more important than it is now.

Social class has a big influence on people's lives

Have a look at p.9 for more on the different social classes in the novel.

1) Most of the characters in *Pride and Prejudice* are upper class — either aristocracy (like Lady Catherine) or gentry (like Darcy, the Bingleys and the Bennets). However, there are lots of little differences based on how rich they are, where their money came from, and how far back they can trace their family.

2) Minor distinctions like these don't stop characters socialising — Lady Catherine has Elizabeth to dinner. But there are strong views about 'marrying down' — Lady Catherine doesn't want her to marry Darcy, and at first he also says it's a "degradation".

> **Writer's Techniques**
>
> Austen's exploration of social class is limited because she only writes about what she experienced. She doesn't write very much about working-class characters like servants.

3) Characters often focus more on wealth and class than personality. E.g. Mrs Bennet wants Bingley to marry one of her daughters before she's even met him, just because he's rich.

Different characters' social manners show their personality

1) The ways that characters respond to social rules give clues about what they're like as a person:

> Miss Bingley thinks social rules and "decorum" are very important — she's insecure about her class status because her family's money comes from trade.

> Mr Collins ignores a social rule when he speaks to Darcy before being introduced. He thinks he's "equal... with the highest rank in the kingdom" because he's a clergyman. This shows how conceited he is.

2) Some characters' personalities are developed by showing how they treat people from a lower social class:

> Mr Darcy is kind and generous to his servants. Although he is proud of his own social status, he isn't mean to other people just because they're from a lower class than he is.

> Lady Catherine encourages flattery and obedience from anyone of a lower class — this highlights her arrogance.

The Bennets are upper class with middle-class connections

1) Austen gives the Bennet sisters an awkward social position as a way of exploring the prejudices of society:

- They are technically the social equals of Darcy, because Mr Bennet is a gentleman.

- But their mother's middle-class background and "low connections" are judged by Darcy and others to "materially lessen their chance of marrying men of any consideration in the world".

© AF archive / Alamy

2) Darcy's prejudice against Elizabeth's class connections is one of the obstacles he has to overcome. He eventually learns that intelligence and manners are more important than social background. This is shown through his relationship with the Gardiners — he realises that they're well-bred and intelligent despite being from a lower class.

Social Class

There's a strong message about social class in the novel — Austen shows that it causes a lot of prejudice...

Austen criticises judgements based on social class

1) Austen criticises the way that social status is used to make <u>assumptions</u> about characters' <u>personalities</u> and manners.

2) Class prejudices mean some characters believe the <u>worst</u> of anyone from a <u>lower</u> social class. For example, when Miss Bingley talks about Wickham's "infamous" behaviour, she says "considering his <u>descent</u>, one could not expect much better." (Wickham's father was <u>employed</u> as a steward at Pemberley.)

© Focus/Everett/Rex Features

3) Similarly, <u>wealth</u> and <u>social status</u> impress some of the characters so much that they're willing to forgive <u>rudeness</u>. For example, Charlotte Lucas doesn't mind Mr Darcy's <u>proud manners</u> because "with <u>family</u>, <u>fortune</u>, everything in his favour... he has a <u>right</u> to be proud."

4) By stating Charlotte's views so <u>straightforwardly</u>, Austen makes the reader <u>wonder</u> if anyone has a <u>right</u> to be proud of something that they <u>haven't worked</u> for — like <u>inherited</u> wealth. Darcy hasn't <u>earned</u> his money — he was just born into the <u>right family</u>.

Austen uses satire to mock class prejudice

Character — Mrs Bennet

Both Lady Catherine and Mrs Bennet are <u>rude</u> and <u>embarrass</u> their families. These <u>similarities</u> emphasise Austen's message that there's no real <u>difference</u> between people <u>with</u> status and wealth and those <u>without</u>.

1) Austen <u>mocks</u> class prejudice by creating <u>characters</u> who show that behaviour is down to <u>personality</u>, not <u>class</u>.

2) Lady Catherine has the <u>highest</u> social status of all the characters. She and her daughter come from a long line of <u>aristocrats</u>. The reader expects them to be <u>respectable</u>, <u>polite</u> and <u>dignified</u>.

3) Austen <u>satirises</u> this expectation by making Lady Catherine the <u>rudest</u>, most <u>arrogant</u> and <u>unpleasant</u> character in the novel. Anne is "<u>sickly</u> and cross", and neither of them are <u>intelligent</u> or <u>interesting</u>.

4) The satire is <u>developed</u> through other characters' <u>treatment</u> of the de Bourghs. The <u>foolish</u> characters are <u>awed</u> and amazed by them:

See p.55 for more on satire.

- <u>Mr Collins</u> treats them with "<u>extraordinary deference</u>".
- When Lady Catherine visits Longbourn she <u>rudely insults</u> the Bennets, but <u>Mrs Bennet</u> is still "<u>flattered</u>" and thinks Lady Catherine is very "<u>civil</u>".

5) The characters that the reader is most likely to <u>sympathise with</u>, such as Elizabeth and Mr Bennet, are openly <u>critical</u> of this attitude. For example, Mr Bennet <u>sarcastically</u> tells Mr Collins that he should be nicer to <u>Darcy</u> than Lady Catherine, because Darcy "has <u>more</u> to <u>give</u>".

"such a father and mother, and such low connections"

Social class is everything in this novel — the fact that the Bennet sisters have a couple of middle-class relatives is enough to damage their marriage prospects. Austen uses the novel to challenge this situation.

Reputation

A bad reputation means that no-one will want to marry you, which is the end of the world in this novel.

Reputation is more important for women than for men

1) The reputations of the <u>female</u> characters are more <u>important</u> than men's and more <u>vulnerable</u> to <u>criticism</u>.

2) Georgiana's almost-elopement is <u>concealed</u> to save her reputation — even though it means allowing Wickham to go <u>unpunished</u>. This shows that <u>reputation</u> is more important than <u>justice</u>.

3) The neighbourhood <u>gossips</u> are disappointed when Wickham marries Lydia — if he hadn't, she might have been forced to "come upon the town" (become a <u>prostitute</u>) or be "<u>secluded</u> from the world". Her reputation would be <u>ruined</u> and she wouldn't be able to live a <u>happy</u> or <u>respectable</u> life.

4) In <u>contrast</u>, Wickham would suffer some "<u>disgrace</u> in the <u>corps</u>", but his reputation wouldn't be <u>permanently damaged</u>.

© News (UK) Ltd/Rex Features

Reputations aren't always deserved

1) Austen uses the <u>contrasting characters</u> of Darcy and Wickham to <u>criticise</u> the way reputations are based on shallow factors. As Elizabeth says: "one has got all the <u>goodness</u>, and the other all the <u>appearance</u> of it":

- Darcy is unsociable, which gives him a <u>reputation</u> with the local people for being <u>cold</u> and <u>rude</u>.
- Wickham is <u>charming</u>, so everyone assumes he has "every <u>virtue</u>".

2) By the end, their <u>true characters</u> are revealed, and they each get the reputation they <u>deserve</u>. Austen shows that reputations should be based on a <u>proper</u> understanding of a person's character.

Family has an important effect on reputation

1) Several events in the novel show how <u>family</u> can affect a person's <u>reputation</u> and chances of <u>marrying well</u>:

- Darcy thinks Bingley shouldn't marry Jane because of her family's "total want of propriety".
- Lydia's scandal would've affected the reputations of all her sisters as "proof of <u>family weakness</u>".
- Darcy <u>saves</u> Lydia's reputation so he can <u>marry Elizabeth</u> — he couldn't marry into her <u>family</u> otherwise.

2) Austen uses these events to show that reputations can be gained <u>unfairly</u> — Jane and Elizabeth's reputations and chances for happiness are <u>threatened</u> by things they have <u>no control</u> over.

Pay attention to the structure of the novel...

You can write about how cleverly the novel is structured — Austen sets up reputations for characters, and then reveals that they're wrong later on. She's criticising society's way of judging people on reputation alone.

Pride and Prejudice

The themes of 'pride' and 'prejudice' keep on popping up through the novel. They even made it into the title.

Austen shows that pride can be positive or negative

1) Lady Catherine's pride in her title and wealth is <u>negative</u> because it makes her <u>rude</u>, <u>arrogant</u> and <u>snobbish</u>.

2) But Darcy's pride in Pemberley "led him to be <u>liberal</u> and <u>generous</u>" to his tenants, and his <u>brotherly</u> pride made him a "<u>kind</u> and careful guardian of his sister". This shows pride can be a <u>positive</u> character trait.

> **Character —Darcy**
>
> Darcy's proposal to Elizabeth is "not more eloquent on the subject of <u>tenderness</u> than of <u>pride</u>". This shows his biggest flaw isn't pride, it's that he cares about pride <u>more</u> than love.

© Everett Collection/Rex Features

Elizabeth and Darcy both show pride and prejudice

1) <u>Pride</u> and <u>prejudice</u> are flaws that Elizabeth and Darcy have to <u>overcome</u> in the course of their <u>relationship</u>:

Pride	Prejudice
• Darcy "<u>mortified</u>" Elizabeth's <u>pride</u> by refusing to dance with her — this means her first impressions of him are negative. • Elizabeth's <u>proud</u> of her <u>ability</u> to <u>judge character</u> — so she <u>stubbornly</u> sticks to her opinion of him. • Darcy's <u>pride</u> in his <u>social status</u> makes him think Elizabeth is <u>beneath</u> him — this makes his behaviour <u>rude</u> and <u>insulting</u>.	• Elizabeth is <u>prejudiced</u> against Darcy and <u>blind</u> to Wickham's true qualities. The <u>narrative</u> follows her <u>point of view</u>, so her prejudices aren't always clear to the <u>reader</u>. • Darcy is <u>prejudiced</u> against anyone of a lower class, and doesn't think anyone outside his <u>own social circle</u> is worth bothering with. This means he thinks all Elizabeth's relatives are <u>inferior</u>.

2) By <u>pointing out</u> each other's <u>pride</u> and <u>prejudice</u>, they're able to <u>overcome</u> these flaws. E.g. Elizabeth accuses Darcy of "<u>arrogance</u>", which makes him see that his behaviour has been <u>rude</u> and <u>ungentlemanly</u>. His letter makes her see that her <u>early impressions</u> of his character were <u>unfair</u>.

Prejudice is widespread in the novel

Most of the characters show <u>prejudice</u> at some point, and Austen shows how <u>damaging</u> it can be, e.g.

1) Prejudice about <u>social class</u> makes Miss Bingley <u>cruel</u> and Mr Collins a <u>ridiculous sycophant</u> (suck up).

2) People in Meryton are prejudiced about <u>social manners</u>, which means they <u>trust</u> Wickham too easily.

KEY QUOTE

"she had been blind, partial, prejudiced, absurd."
Most of the characters in the novel have some social and personal prejudices, but it's Elizabeth and Darcy who change their attitudes the most — they <u>realise</u> that they've been prejudiced against one another.

Practice Questions

You know the drill by now — it's time to test yourself and see what you've learned about themes. Nothing too hard to begin with, just some quick questions to see if you're awake and alert. In fact, some of these you should be able to answer in your sleep, so snuggle down and let's begin...

Quick Questions

1) Which of these characters is open about falling in love and which keeps her feelings to herself?
   a) Jane   b) Lydia

2) Is Lydia's love for Wickham based on:
   a) an understanding of his true character   or   b) shallow attraction?

3) Give two examples of unhappy marriages in *Pride and Prejudice*.

4) Why does Mrs Bennet think Jane's engagement will help her other daughters marry well?

5) Are the Bennet family:
   a) Middle class with working-class connections
   b) Working class with upper-class connections
   c) Upper class with middle-class connections?

6) Name two characters who Austen uses to mock class prejudice.

7) Why is Darcy reluctant to tell anyone about Wickham's attempted elopement with Georgiana?

8) Whose reputation is described in the following quote?
   "He is not at all liked in Hertfordshire. Everybody is disgusted with his pride."

9) Name one character who is prejudiced, and say who or what they're prejudiced against.

10) Give one example of how Darcy shows that pride can sometimes be positive.

Practice Questions

Now on to the tougher stuff — but hopefully not too tough. You don't need to write long essay answers to these questions, but that doesn't mean you can rush through them either. Take your time and use them to get you thinking carefully about the book and its themes.

In-depth Questions

1) "The 'pride' in *Pride and Prejudice* refers to Darcy, while the 'prejudice' is shown by Elizabeth." Do you think this statement is true? Explain your answer.

2) How is Elizabeth and Darcy's relationship different from Lydia and Wickham's?

3) Explain why the following characters decide to get married, using examples from the text.
   a) Jane Bennet   b) Mr Collins   c) Charlotte Lucas.

4) Do you think Jane Austen thought it was fair that people's reputations could be damaged if they didn't conform to social rules? Give reasons for your answer.

5) Which character best shows that romance isn't enough for a happy marriage? Explain your answer.

6) Elizabeth thinks that Charlotte shouldn't have married Mr Collins. Do you agree with her? Explain your answer.

7) How does Austen use humour to get across her opinion on class prejudice? Explain your answer.

8) What effect does Lydia have on the reputations of Jane and Elizabeth? How fair do you think this is?

Practice Questions

And just when you thought you'd finished... here are some proper, industrial-strength, exam-type questions. Don't say I never give you anything (but feel free to say I never give you anything you want).

Exam-style Questions

1) Using the extract below as a starting point, how does Austen present different characters' attitudes towards marriage in the novel?

> "Your plan is a good one," replied Elizabeth, "where nothing is in question but the desire of being well married, and if I were determined to get a rich husband, or any husband, I dare say I should adopt it. But these are not Jane's feelings; she is not acting by design. As yet, she cannot even be certain of the degree of her own regard nor of its reasonableness. She has known him only a fortnight. She danced four dances with him at Meryton; she saw him one morning at his own house, and has since dined with him in company four times. This is not quite enough to make her understand his character."
>
> "Not as you represent it. Had she merely *dined* with him, she might only have discovered whether he had a good appetite; but you must remember that four evenings have also been spent together — and four evenings may do a great deal."
>
> "Yes; these four evenings have enabled them to ascertain that they both like Vingt-un better than Commerce; but with respect to any other leading characteristic, I do not imagine that much has been unfolded."
>
> "Well," said Charlotte, "I wish Jane success with all my heart; and if she were married to him to-morrow, I should think she had as good a chance of happiness as if she were to be studying his character for a twelvemonth. Happiness in marriage is entirely a matter of chance. If the dispositions of the parties are ever so well known to each other or ever so similar beforehand, it does not advance their felicity in the least. They always continue to grow sufficiently unlike afterwards to have their share of vexation; and it is better to know as little as possible of the defects of the person with whom you are to pass your life."
>
> "You make me laugh, Charlotte; but it is not sound. You know it is not sound, and that you would never act in this way yourself."

2) How does Austen present differences in social class as an influence on people's lives in *Pride and Prejudice*?

3) How does the theme of love create interest in the novel?

4) How does Jane Austen present ideas about reputation in *Pride and Prejudice*?

The Structure of 'Pride and Prejudice'

Oh good, a page on structure — it's nice to start off a new section on a firm foundation, I always think.

The novel has four main phases

© Moviestore collection Ltd / Alamy

Pride and Prejudice has the basic structure of a typical romance novel and moves through four main phases:

1) The hero and heroine (Elizabeth and Darcy) meet.

2) At first, the heroine dislikes and misjudges the hero.

3) The characters' true qualities are gradually revealed.

4) The hero and heroine are eventually united.

There are lots of different interlinking stories

1) The novel is made more complex and interesting by the other stories running through it — e.g. the romance between Bingley and Jane, Mr Collins's search for a wife and the revelations about Wickham.

2) The obstacles that Darcy and Elizabeth have to overcome to find love also liven things up. They have to sort out their initial poor opinion of each other, and also issues of:

- social class and the disapproval of family and friends.

- scandal and embarrassment (e.g. Lydia's elopement).

- false information and impressions (e.g. Wickham's lies about Darcy).

- their own character flaws and assumptions about one another.

The book's title — 'Pride and Prejudice' — points out two of the character flaws that keep Elizabeth and Darcy apart.

The novel has a symmetrical structure

1) The events of *Pride and Prejudice* happen over one year.

2) The novel has a basically symmetrical structure. The meeting at Pemberley is the turning point in Elizabeth and Darcy's relationship, and the main obstacles to the relationship are mirrored on either side of it:

| Darcy is interested in Elizabeth but she thinks he's proud and arrogant. It seems as if they can never be together because of this barrier. | The meeting at Pemberley brings them together. | Elizabeth now likes Darcy but the social shame of Lydia's elopement means Darcy can't associate with Elizabeth's family. Again, it seems as if they can never be together. |

3) At the end of the novel, Darcy fixes the problem of Lydia's elopement, and is finally united with Elizabeth.

KEY QUOTE

"They owed the restoration of Lydia... to him."

OK, paying Wickham to marry Lydia isn't quite as heroic as rescuing someone from a burning building, but it proves how much Darcy loves Elizabeth. It's also important in bringing the novel to a happy conclusion.

Language — How the Characters Speak

The formal way the characters speak in *Pride and Prejudice* can be off-putting at first, but stick with it.

Dialogue helps to develop the characters

There's not much <u>description</u> of the characters. Instead, Austen uses their <u>language</u> to show what they're <u>like</u>:

1) Lydia's speech is full of <u>exclamation marks</u> and <u>immature</u> remarks — "<u>Lord!</u> how I <u>laughed!</u>", "Mrs Forster and me are <u>such friends!</u>"— this makes her seem <u>excitable</u> and <u>silly</u>.

2) Lady Catherine's language shows that she is <u>rude</u> and <u>arrogant</u>. E.g. she calls Elizabeth an "obstinate, headstrong girl!" and <u>demands</u> "do you know who I am?"

This page gives a few key examples of different characters' language, but remember that language is important for all the characters — not just the ones mentioned here.

Characters' language is often restricted by social rules

1) <u>Strict conventions</u> about what is <u>polite</u> mean that the characters can't always <u>say</u> what they really <u>think</u>. How different characters <u>adapt</u> their language within these <u>social rules</u> reveals a lot about their <u>personality</u>.

2) Elizabeth is <u>clever</u> enough to express her <u>opinion</u> without being <u>rude</u>. E.g. when she says Darcy allows "nothing for the influence of <u>friendship</u> and <u>affection</u>" she's <u>subtly</u> accusing him of being <u>cold</u>.

3) But <u>Mrs Bennet</u> is too <u>stupid</u> to express herself <u>politely</u>. She criticises Darcy very <u>obviously</u> by talking about people who "never open their <u>mouths</u>".

© Everett Collection/Rex Features

Austen uses speech to show changing relationships in the novel

1) Some characters' language <u>changes</u> depending on their <u>intentions</u>. For example, Mr Collins only <u>flatters</u> people when he has something to <u>gain</u> from <u>complimenting</u> them — the way he talks to the Bennets <u>changes</u> when he no longer hopes to <u>marry</u> one of the daughters:

• At first he sounds <u>very eager</u> to please the Bennets — he <u>apologises</u> for "injuring your <u>amiable</u> <u>daughters</u>" by being the next in line to inherit, and <u>compliments</u> them on having "so <u>fine</u> a <u>family</u>".

• In contrast, his language after Lydia's scandal is <u>judgemental</u> and <u>unforgiving</u>. He <u>blames</u> Mr Bennet for "a <u>faulty degree</u> of <u>indulgence</u>" and advises him to "throw off your unworthy child".

2) Darcy's changing language shows how his relationship with Elizabeth develops. At first he <u>refuses</u> to speak to anyone outside of "<u>his own party</u>". In time, he's more <u>comfortable</u> with Elizabeth and starts to <u>join in</u> with her witty banter, for example asking her "Do you talk by rule, then, while you are dancing?" By the <u>end</u>, his language is more <u>passionate</u> — he calls her "<u>dearest</u>, <u>loveliest</u> Elizabeth!"

EXAM TIP

Write about how Austen uses dialogue to create characters...

Austen uses lots of dialogue, so it's important that you get to grips with what the characters mean and what their speech says about them. It'll help you to make intelligent points about their personalities in the exam.

Language — Irony and Satire

Jane Austen is a funny writer. She uses irony and satire to poke fun at her characters and at society itself.

Austen uses different types of irony

Austen creates <u>humour</u> in *Pride and Prejudice* by using <u>irony</u> — saying the <u>opposite</u> of what she <u>really means</u>, or pointing out the <u>difference</u> between how things <u>seem</u> and how they <u>are</u>. Austen's use of irony is <u>funny</u>, but <u>also</u> makes the reader think <u>seriously</u> about <u>problems</u> in society.

© WORKING TITLE / THE KOBAL COLLECTION / BAILEY, ALEX

Irony in Dialogue

- Some characters use irony <u>deliberately</u>. Elizabeth <u>mocks</u> Darcy for being unsociable — "nobody can ever be introduced in a ball-room." She means the <u>opposite</u> — it's perfectly acceptable to be introduced in a ballroom.
- Some are ironic <u>without realising</u>. After Lydia and Wickham's marriage, Mr Collins says that Mr Bennet should "forgive them as a Christian, but never to admit them in your sight". His advice isn't forgiving or Christian.

Narrative Irony

The <u>narrator</u> often says the opposite of what she really means. E.g. when Jane's ill, the narrator says the Bingley sisters "were miserable" and "solaced their wretchedness... by duets". Austen means that they <u>weren't</u> miserable — they easily forgot and sang duets instead.

Situational Irony

The irony comes from the <u>situation</u> the characters are in. E.g. it's ironic that Darcy persuades <u>Bingley</u> not to marry <u>Jane Bennet</u> because of her "objectionable" <u>family</u>, but then <u>proposes</u> to <u>Elizabeth Bennet</u> himself.

Irony in Character

The characters' <u>personalities</u> provide irony. For example, it's ironic that Wickham appears to be a <u>brave</u>, dashing <u>hero</u> but turns out to be the <u>villain</u>, and that Darcy seems <u>rude</u> and <u>unpleasant</u> but turns out to be the novel's <u>hero</u>.

Austen uses satire to point out things she doesn't like

<u>Satire</u> means commenting on the <u>shortcomings</u> or <u>stupidity</u> of people or society by making a <u>joke</u> of them.

1) Austen uses <u>Lady Catherine</u> to satirise the aristocracy. She's a <u>caricature</u> — her character is <u>exaggerated</u> beyond what's realistic to make her funnier. She's the most "<u>insolent</u> and <u>disagreeable</u>" character in the novel, yet the aristocracy were meant to be more <u>polite</u> and <u>respectable</u> than anyone else.

Theme — Social Class

Austen uses <u>satire</u> to point out things that seem <u>stupid</u> or <u>wrong</u>. E.g. She uses Mr Collins's <u>blind admiration</u> for Lady Catherine to satirise society's habit of valuing wealth and status <u>more</u> than <u>personality</u>.

2) Austen also mocks the <u>neighbourhood gossips</u> in Longbourn by making fun of the way they make <u>instant</u>, <u>shallow judgements</u> about people, then <u>change</u> their minds very quickly. For example, when they find out Darcy's <u>rich</u> he's "much <u>handsomer</u> than Mr Bingley", but when he <u>won't dance</u> he is "<u>unworthy</u> to be <u>compared</u> with his friend".

Comment on why Austen uses irony and satire...

It's all part of her criticism of society in the novel as a whole. Don't take anything that Austen says at face value — if you look harder, you'll often find she means just the opposite. Confusing... but hilarious.

The Writing Style of 'Pride and Prejudice'

Coming up: a most impressive term that you can use to amaze your friends and confound your enemies. Or, even better, use it in your exam... the omniscient narrator. Oooh...

The novel has an omniscient narrator

1) *Pride and Prejudice* has an <u>omniscient narrator</u> — the writer <u>knows everything</u> that's going on in the story, so they can fill you in on details that you wouldn't know if one of the <u>characters</u> was narrating it.

2) An omniscient narrator is more <u>trustworthy</u> than a <u>first-person</u> narrator — the reader can <u>believe</u> everything the narrator tells them without worrying that their opinion might be <u>biased</u>.

3) The narrator is <u>separate</u> from Elizabeth, but the story follows her most closely, and you see most events from <u>her viewpoint</u>. You know a lot of her inner thoughts compared with other characters.

4) Austen usually reveals the <u>inner thoughts</u> of <u>other</u> characters through <u>letters</u> instead of the narrative voice. E.g. <u>Mr Darcy's</u> feelings after Elizabeth <u>rejects</u> him are shown in the letter he writes her.

5) You can sometimes guess Austen's <u>own views</u>. The tone of <u>disapproval</u> when Lady Catherine is introduced suggests that Austen <u>doesn't like</u> the idea of someone from a higher social class making people feel inferior.

> "Her air was <u>not conciliating</u>, nor was her manner of receiving them such as to make her visitors <u>forget their inferior rank</u>."

Jane Austen is a realist

1) <u>Realism</u> is a type of writing where the author aims to give an <u>accurate picture</u> of life as it really is.

2) Austen is usually called a realist because the <u>issues</u> in the novel are ones that really <u>affected people</u> during the period when it was written.

The Society Shown in *Pride and Prejudice*

Austen may be a realist, but that <u>doesn't</u> mean she gives us a complete picture of life at the time. She <u>doesn't</u> tackle any of the <u>grittier issues</u> such as war, politics or poverty. She only describes her <u>own experience</u>, which is <u>upper middle class</u> and <u>sheltered</u>.

3) The characters are <u>based</u> on people you might have met if you'd been around in those days, but sometimes Austen <u>exaggerates</u> their personality traits, usually to make them <u>funnier</u>. For example, <u>Mrs Bennet</u> is a '<u>caricature</u>' character (see p.31) — she has an <u>exaggerated obsession</u> with eligible bachelors and marriage, but this highlights the <u>real concern</u> of a mother trying to marry her daughters well.

4) The <u>scandal</u> caused by Lydia's elopement gives a <u>realistic</u> view of how people would <u>react</u> during the period. On the other hand, <u>not everyone</u> who got themselves into a situation like this would have a wealthy man like Mr Darcy to <u>rescue</u> them from it. It's a <u>romanticised version</u> of a realistic situation.

"He was the proudest, most disagreeable man in the world"

Don't take everything in the narrative at face value. This quote is the opinion of the ball-goers in Chapter 3 of Mr Darcy — it doesn't mean that Austen really believes Darcy is the most disagreeable man in the world.

Motifs and Symbols in 'Pride and Prejudice'

Jane Austen uses some writer's tricks to help her tell the story...

Places represent the people who live there

The events of *Pride and Prejudice* take place in <u>different locations</u> — these different settings seem to <u>reflect</u> the personality of the <u>characters</u> associated with that place:

Longbourn symbolises Mr and Mrs Bennet

- The name "Longbourn" suggests it's a <u>negative</u> place — it sounds like a <u>burden</u> that's been <u>borne</u> (put up with) for a <u>long</u> time. This reflects the Bennets' <u>marriage</u>.

- The Bennet sisters always seem <u>pleased</u> to <u>leave</u> Longbourn — Elizabeth thinks her Lake District trip will give her "<u>fresh life</u>" and Lydia is in "<u>restless ecstasy</u>" about Brighton. This suggests that they've outgrown their parents and feel <u>restricted</u> by them.

Meryton symbolises Kitty and Lydia

- The name "Meryton" makes it sound <u>social</u> and <u>fun</u> — it's a <u>merry</u> town.

- <u>Balls</u> are hosted there and it's full of <u>soldiers</u>. This reflects Kitty and Lydia's <u>flirtatious</u> ways.

- There's also a "milliner's" (a hat shop), that Kitty and Lydia visit "three or four times a week". This represents their <u>shallowness</u>.

Pemberley symbolises Mr Darcy

- Austen writes about Pemberley in <u>unusual detail</u>, and it's really <u>positive</u> — she uses words like "<u>handsome</u>" and "<u>remarkable</u>". Pemberley is <u>genuine</u> as well as beautiful — "neither formal, nor falsely adorned".

- This all suggests that Darcy has good <u>taste</u> and that, like his home, he's "without any <u>artificial</u> appearance".

- Elizabeth's growing "<u>delight</u>" at Pemberley shows that her <u>opinion</u> of <u>Darcy</u> himself is becoming more <u>positive</u>.

Rosings symbolises Lady Catherine

- Rosings is <u>showy</u> but <u>tasteless</u> — the furniture has "<u>splendour</u>" but not "<u>elegance</u>". This echoes Lady Catherine's <u>arrogance</u> and lack of social grace.

- It's a <u>boring</u> place — Colonel Fitzwilliam finds that "<u>anything</u> was a welcome relief to him at <u>Rosings</u>". This mirrors Lady Catherine's boring, self-obsessed personality.

Austen contrasts indoors and outdoors

1) There's a noticeable <u>difference</u> between how characters act <u>indoors</u> and <u>outdoors</u>.

2) Inside parlours and ballrooms, the characters tend to be <u>restricted</u> by <u>social conventions</u>. But when they're <u>outside</u>, the characters' behaviour and speech are more <u>free</u> and <u>open</u>. E.g.

> At the <u>end</u> of the novel when Darcy visits Elizabeth, he is "<u>silent</u>, grave and <u>indifferent</u>" inside the house. But when they're out <u>walking</u> he <u>openly</u> tells Elizabeth "I thought only of you".

© AF archive / Alamy

3) This means many of the <u>dramatic events</u> happen <u>outdoors</u> — e.g. Darcy gives Elizabeth his <u>revealing letter</u> in a "<u>grove</u>" (a small wood) and Lady Catherine <u>argues</u> with Elizabeth about Darcy in a "little <u>wilderness</u>".

Character — Elizabeth

Elizabeth is <u>linked</u> to the <u>outdoors</u>, which shows that her character is <u>lively</u> and <u>natural</u>. She's <u>comfortable</u> and <u>confident</u> when in nature — she's described on walks "<u>jumping</u> over stiles" and "<u>rejoicing</u> as she rambled about".

Motifs and Symbols in 'Pride and Prejudice'

My English teacher used to waffle on about how Austen can make the arrival of a letter as dramatic as a bomb going off. I wouldn't go quite that far, but she does use letters and journeys to add excitement to the novel.

Journeys symbolise change

1) Journeys release characters from the restrictions they have in one setting and let them act more freely.

2) Because of this, journeys act as catalysts (causes) for change, and usually lead to dramatic plot twists. E.g.

   - Journeys often mark a turning point in the plot. When Elizabeth goes to Hunsford she gets an offer of marriage and when she goes on holiday with the Gardiners she meets Darcy again.

   - Darcy proposes to Elizabeth when she's away from Longbourn because he finds it easier to forget her family's embarrassing behaviour when they're not "immediately before" him.

3) Austen sometimes uses journeys to symbolise a character's changing attitude. E.g.

   - Darcy travels to London to bribe Wickham, in order to save Elizabeth from pain and scandal. He despises Wickham, and has to overcome his pride before he can pay off Wickham.

   - Darcy's journey represents his dramatic change from a character who was "ate up with pride" to someone who realises that love and happiness are more important than pride.

Letters develop characterisation and plot

1) Austen uses letters to show the voice and inner thoughts of a character. For example, even before Mr Collins arrives, his letter to Mr Bennet shows that he's "pompous".

2) Characters express themselves more honestly in letters than face to face. Darcy only feels able to explain the Wickham story in a letter, where he can control what "ought to be revealed".

Context — Women in Regency Society
The women's reliance on letters in the novel emphasises the restrictions society placed on them. For example, Elizabeth and Jane have to wait at home for letters for news of Lydia's elopement.

3) Letters also introduce new information about characters and events that move the plot along. E.g. when Jane sends a letter about Lydia's elopement, it creates a new obstacle to keep Darcy and Elizabeth apart.

4) The characters' reactions to various letters are often as important as the letters themselves. For example:

© AF archive / Alamy

   - When Elizabeth reads the letter about Lydia's elopement in front of Darcy, her reaction is dramatic — she "trembled", was "breathless" and looked "miserably ill".

   - Darcy's reaction creates more suspense — he walks about in "earnest meditation". The reader has no idea how Darcy really feels about the scandal or how it will change his relationship with Elizabeth.

(EXAM TIP) *Link letters to the novel's context...*

Letters were a crucial method of communication in Regency times, which helps to explain why they're so important in the novel. Austen also uses them as a tool to add dramatic moments to the narrative.

Practice Questions

Just for a change, this section is going to end with some questions. I know, it's a daring move.

Quick Questions

1) Describe the four main phases of the novel's structure.

2) Does Lydia's speech make her seem:
   a) pompous and boring   b) lively and witty   c) excitable and silly

3) Give a definition of each of the following:
   a) irony   b) satire.

4) *Pride and Prejudice* has an omniscient narrator. What does this mean?

5) Give one example of a character who seems more comfortable outdoors than indoors.

6) Who proposes to Elizabeth during her trip to Kent?

In-depth Questions

1) How do you think the symmetrical structure of *Pride and Prejudice* emphasises the importance of the accidental meeting between Darcy and Elizabeth at Pemberley.

2) "There is irony in the speech of both Mr and Mrs Bennet, but of different kinds."
   Do you agree or disagree with the above statement? Explain your answer.

3) Explain how Jane Austen satirises the character of Lady Catherine de Bourgh.
   What do you think this says about Austen's own opinion of the aristocracy?

4) Do you think Jane Austen was a realist? Explain your answer using evidence from the text of *Pride and Prejudice*.

5) How are Elizabeth's changing feelings towards Darcy symbolised by the places in which she sees him?

6) Which letter do you think causes the most drama and excitement in *Pride and Prejudice*? Explain your answer.

Practice Questions

These questions should help avoid nasty surprises in the exam.

Exam-style Questions

1) Using the extract below as a starting point, explore Austen's use of humour in the novel.

> ...they conversed with so much spirit and flow, as to draw the attention of Lady Catherine herself, as well as of Mr. Darcy. His eyes had been soon and repeatedly turned towards them with a look of curiosity; and that her ladyship, after a while, shared the feeling, was more openly acknowledged, for she did not scruple to call out:
>
> "What is that you are saying, Fitzwilliam? What is it you are talking of? What are you telling Miss Bennet? Let me hear what it is."
>
> "We are speaking of music, madam," said he, when no longer able to avoid a reply.
>
> "Of music! Then pray speak aloud. It is of all subjects my delight. I must have my share in the conversation if you are speaking of music. There are few people in England, I suppose, who have more true enjoyment of music than myself, or a better natural taste. If I had ever learnt, I should have been a great proficient. And so would Anne, if her health had allowed her to apply. I am confident that she would have performed delightfully. How does Georgiana get on, Darcy?"
>
> Mr. Darcy spoke with affectionate praise of his sister's proficiency.
>
> "I am very glad to hear such a good account of her," said Lady Catherine; "and pray tell her from me, that she cannot expect to excel if she does not practice a good deal."
>
> "I assure you, madam," he replied, "that she does not need such advice. She practises very constantly."
>
> "So much the better. It cannot be done too much; and when I next write to her, I shall charge her not to neglect it on any account. I often tell young ladies that no excellence in music is to be acquired without constant practice. I have told Miss Bennet several times, that she will never play really well unless she practises more; and though Mrs. Collins has no instrument, she is very welcome, as I have often told her, to come to Rosings every day, and play on the pianoforte in Mrs. Jenkinson's room. She would be in nobody's way, you know, in that part of the house."

2) Show how Austen uses speech to bring out the different personalities of Mr and Mrs Bennet.

3) How does Jane Austen make you feel differently about the attitudes and behaviour of Mr Darcy in two different chapters of the novel?

4) How does Austen make Mr Collins a figure that everyone will laugh at?
   Support your answer with details from the novel.

Exam Preparation

Getting to know the text will put you at a massive advantage in the exam. It's not enough just to read it though — you've got to get to grips with the nitty-gritty bits. It's all about gathering evidence...

The exam questions will test four main skills

You will need to show the examiner that you can:

1) Write about the text in a thoughtful way — picking out appropriate examples and quotations to back up your opinions.

2) Identify and explain features of the book's form, structure and language. Show how Austen uses these to create meanings and effects.

> Not all exam boards will test you on this. Check with your teacher.

3) Link the novel to its cultural, social and historical background (i.e. Regency England).

4) Write in a clear, well-structured way. 5% of the marks in your English Literature exams are for spelling, punctuation and grammar. Make sure that your writing is as accurate as possible.

Preparation is important

1) It's important to cover all the different sections of this book in your revision. You need to make sure you understand the text's context, plot, characters, themes and writer's techniques.

2) In the exam, you'll need to bring together your ideas about these topics to answer the question quickly.

3) Think about the different characters and themes in the text, and write down some key points and ideas about each one. Then, find some evidence to support each point — this could be something from any of the sections in this book. You could set out your evidence in a table like this:

Theme: Marriage	
Practicality	Charlotte Lucas needs to marry for financial security. She doesn't love Mr Collins, but it's an "eligible match".
Marrying for love	Elizabeth rejects Darcy and Mr Collins — she wants to marry for love rather than for practical reasons.
Personality	Austen suggests that this is the most important factor in a marriage. Mr and Mrs Bennet have little in common and are frustrated with one another.
Social expectations	Society expects that women will get married. Lydia thinks it's embarrassing to be an "old maid".
Social status	Mrs Bennet thinks Jane's marriage will be a "promising thing for her younger daughters" — it might help them be introduced to potential suitable husbands (preferably wealthy ones).

Preparing to succeed — a cunning plot indeed...

Knowing the plot inside out will be unbelievably helpful in the exam. It'll help you to stay calm and make sure you write a brilliant answer that positively glitters with little gems of evidence. The exam's just a chance for you to show off...

The Exam Question

This page deals with how to approach an exam question. The stuff below will help you get started on a scorching exam answer, more scorching than, say, a phoenix cooking fiery fajitas in a flaming furnace.

Read the question carefully and underline key words

1) The style of question you'll get depends on which exam board you're taking.

2) Read all the instructions carefully. Make sure you know how many questions you need to answer and how much time you should spend answering each one.

3) If the question has more than one part, look at the total number of marks for each bit. This should help you to plan your time in the exam.

4) Read the question at least twice so you completely understand it. Underline the key words. If you're given an extract, underline important words or phrases in that too.

Henry didn't read the weather report carefully enough when planning his weekend activities.

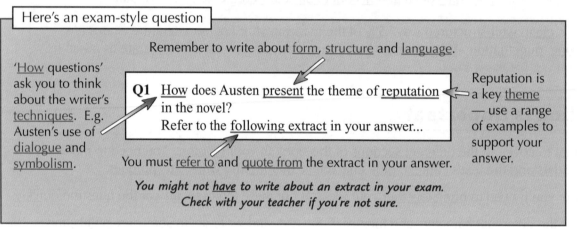

Here's an exam-style question

Remember to write about form, structure and language.

'How questions' ask you to think about the writer's techniques. E.g. Austen's use of dialogue and symbolism.

Q1 How does Austen present the theme of reputation in the novel?
Refer to the following extract in your answer...

Reputation is a key theme — use a range of examples to support your answer.

You must refer to and quote from the extract in your answer.

You might not have to write about an extract in your exam. Check with your teacher if you're not sure.

Get to know exam language

Some words come up time and again in exam questions. Have a look at some specimen questions, pick out words that are often used in questions and make sure that you understand what they mean. You could write a few down whilst you're revising. For example:

Question Word	You need to...
Explore / Explain	Show how the writer deals with a theme, character or idea. Make several different points to answer the question.
How does	Think about the techniques or literary features that the author uses to get their point across.
Give examples	Use direct quotes and describe events from the text in your own words.
Refer to	Read the question so that you know if you need to write about just an extract, or an extract and the rest of the text.

The advice squad — the best cops in the NYPD...

Whatever question you're asked in the exam, your answer should touch on the main characters, themes, structure and language of the text. All the stuff we've covered in the rest of the book in fact. It's so neat, it's almost like we planned it.

Planning Your Answer

I'll say this once — and then I'll probably repeat it several times — it is absolutely, completely, totally and utterly essential that you make a plan before you start writing. Only a fool jumps right in without a plan...

Plan your answer before you start

1) If you plan, you're less likely to forget something <u>important</u>.

2) A good plan will help you <u>organise</u> your ideas — and write a good, <u>well-structured</u> essay.

3) Write your plan at the <u>top of your answer booklet</u> and draw a <u>neat line</u> through it when you've finished.

4) <u>Don't</u> spend <u>too long</u> on your plan. It's only <u>rough work</u>, so you don't need to write in full sentences. Here are a few <u>examples</u> of different ways you can plan your answer:

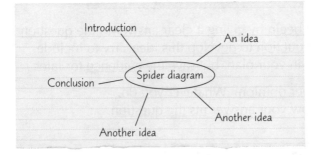

Bullet points...
- Introduction...
- An idea...
- The next idea...
- Another idea...
- Yet another idea...
- Conclusion...

Include bits of evidence in your plan

1) <u>Writing</u> your essay will be much <u>easier</u> if you include <u>important quotes</u> and <u>examples</u> in your plan.

2) You could include them in a <u>table</u> like this one:

3) <u>Don't</u> spend <u>too long</u> writing out quotes though. It's just to make sure you <u>don't forget</u> anything when you write your answer.

A point...	Quote to back this up...
Another point...	Quote...
A different point...	Example...
A brand new point...	Quote...

Structure your answer

Introduction
↓
Middle Section
— paragraphs
expanding
your
argument.
↓
Conclusion

1) Your <u>introduction</u> should give a brief answer to the question you're writing about. Make it clear how you're going to <u>tackle the topic</u>.

2) The <u>middle section</u> of your essay should explain your answer in detail and give evidence to back it up. Write a <u>paragraph</u> for each point you make. Make sure you <u>comment</u> on your evidence and <u>explain how</u> it helps to <u>prove</u> your point.

3) Remember to write a <u>conclusion</u> — a paragraph at the end which <u>sums up</u> your <u>main points</u>. There's <u>more</u> about introductions and conclusions on the <u>next page</u>.

Dirk finally felt ready to tackle the topic.

To plan or not to plan, that is the question...

The answer is yes, yes, a thousand times yes. Often students dive right in, worried that planning will take up valuable time. But 5 minutes spent organising a well-structured answer is loads better than pages of waffle. Mmm waffles.

Writing Introductions and Conclusions

Now you've made that plan that I was banging on about on the last page, you'll know what your main points are. This is going to make writing your introduction and conclusion as easy as pie.

Get to the point straight away in your introduction

1) First, you need to work out what the question is asking you to do:

> How is the character of Lydia important to the novel?
>
> The question is asking you to think about the role of Lydia in the text.
> Plan your essay by thinking about how this character drives the plot forward.

2) When you've planned your essay, you should begin by giving a clear answer to the question in a sentence or two. Use the rest of the introduction to develop this idea. Try to include the main paragraph ideas that you have listed in your plan, but save the evidence for later.

3) You could also use the introduction to give your opinion. Whatever you do, make sure your introduction makes it clear how your answer fits the question.

Your conclusion must answer the question

1) The most important thing you have to do at the end of your writing is to summarise your answer to the question.

2) It's your last chance to persuade the examiner, so make your main point again.

3) Use your last sentence to really impress the examiner — it will make your essay stand out. You could develop your own opinion of the text or highlight which of your points you thought was the most interesting.

The examiner was struggling
to see the answer clearly.

Use the question words in your introduction and conclusion

1) Try to use words or phrases from the question in your introduction and conclusion.

> How does Austen use irony in the novel?

2) This will show the examiner that you're answering the question.

> Austen uses irony in 'Pride and Prejudice' to add humour, but she also uses it to criticise aspects of upper-class society as a whole.

The first line of the introduction gives a clear answer, which will lead on to the rest of the essay.

3) This will also help you keep the question fresh in your mind so your answer doesn't wander off-topic.

I've come to the conclusion that I really like pie...

To conclude, the introduction eases the examiner in gently, whilst the conclusion is your last chance to impress. But remember — the examiner doesn't want to see any new points lurking in those closing sentences.

Writing Main Paragraphs

So we've covered the beginning and the end, now it's time for the meaty bit. The roast beef in between the prawn cocktail and the treacle tart. This page is about how to structure your paragraphs. It's quite simple...

P.E.E.D. is how to put your argument together

Remember to start a new paragraph every time you make a new point.

1) P.E.E.D. stands for: Point, Example, Explain, Develop.

2) Begin each paragraph by making a point. Then give an example from the text (either a quote or a description). Next, explain how your example backs up your point.

3) Finally, try to develop your point by writing about its effect on the reader, how it links to another part of the text or what the writer's intention is in including it.

Use short quotes to support your ideas

1) Don't just use words from the novel to repeat what you've already said...

> Mrs Bennet's greatest wish is to see her children married, because then she won't want anything: "I shall have nothing to wish for."

This just gives an example from the text without offering any explanation or analysis.

2) Instead, it's much better to use short quotes as evidence to support a point you're making.

3) It makes the essay structure clearer and smoother if most quotes are embedded in your sentences.

It's better to use short, embedded quotes as evidence. Then you can go on to explain them.

> Mrs Bennet's greatest wish is to see her children "well married". This emphasises how important marriage is in the upper-class society in which she lives, and hints at how important her daughters' marriages are to her own social standing.

Get to know some literary language

1) Using literary terms in your answer will make your essay stand out — as long as you use them correctly.

2) When you're revising, think about literary terms that are relevant to the text and how you might include them in an essay. Take a look at the table below for some examples.

Literary Term	Definition	Example
Symbolism	When something is used by an author to represent something else.	Pemberley symbolises Mr Darcy — "handsome" and "remarkable".
Hyperbole	Exaggerated language used for emphasis or humour.	"Nobody can tell what I suffer!"
Satire	Using humour to comment on the shortcomings of people or society.	Mr Collins has been appointed as a vicar, but he's humorously unchristian.

This page is so exciting — I nearly...

Now now, let's all be grown-ups and avoid the obvious joke. It's a good way of remembering how to structure your paragraphs though. Point, Example, Explain, Develop. Simple. Maybe we could make a rap or something... anyone?

In the Exam

Keeping cool in the exam can be tricky. But if you take in all the stuff on this page, you'll soon have it down to a fine art. Then you can stroll out of that exam hall with the swagger of an essay-writing master.

Don't panic if you make a mistake

1) Okay, so say you've timed the exam beautifully. Instead of putting your feet up on the desk for the last 5 minutes, it's a good idea to read through your answers and correct any mistakes...

2) If you want to get rid of a mistake, cross it out. Don't scribble it out as this can look messy. Make any corrections neatly and clearly instead of writing on top of the words you've already written.

> techniques
> The author uses various literary ~~teknikues~~ to explore this theme .

This is the clearest way to correct a mistake. Don't be tempted to try writing on top of the original word.

3) If you've left out a word or a phrase and you've got space to add it in above the line it's missing from, write the missing bit above the line with a '∧' to show exactly where it should go.

Re-read the sentence carefully to work out where the '∧' symbol needs to go.

> and hyperbole
> The writer uses imagery to draw attention to this point.

4) If you've left out whole sentences or paragraphs, write them in a separate section at the end of the essay. Put a star (*) next to both the extra writing and the place you want it to go.

Always keep an eye on the time

1) It's surprisingly easy to run out of time in exams. You've got to leave enough time to answer all the questions you're asked to do. You've also got to leave enough time to finish each essay properly — with a clear ending.

2) Here are some tips on how to avoid running out of time:

- Work out how much time you have for each part of your answer before you start.
- Take off a few minutes at the beginning to plan, and a few minutes at the end for your conclusion.
- Make sure you have a watch to time yourself — and keep checking it.
- Be strict with yourself — if you spend too long on one part of your answer, you may run out of time.
- If you're running out of time, keep calm, finish the point you're on and move on to your conclusion.

Stephanie never had a problem with keeping cool.

Treat an exam like a spa day — just relax...

Some people actually do lose the plot when they get into the exam. The trick is to keep calm and well... carry on. If you make sure you get your exam technique sorted, you'll be as relaxed as a sloth in a room full of easy chairs.

Section Six — Exam Advice

Sample Exam Question

And now the bit you've all been waiting for — a sample exam question and a lovely little plan.
Go and make yourself a cup of tea, then settle down and enjoy.

Here's a sample exam question

Read this feisty exam question. That's the best way to start...

> In the exam, you'll be given the full extract in the exam paper.

Read the question carefully. Underline the important bits.

Write about context — how attitudes towards wealth and social class were different in Austen's day from today.

> Q1   In Chapter 29, read the section that begins "From the entrance-hall..." and ends with "...to be exactly what he represented."
>
> Beginning with this passage, write about how differences in wealth and social class are presented as an influence on the behaviour of characters in the novel.

This means you'll need to discuss the passage given in detail, but you also need to refer to the rest of the book.

Focus on examples of how characters behave towards one another, rather than on their situation and lifestyle.

The novel has three social classes — the aristocracy, the landed gentry and the professional middle class.

Here's how you could plan your answer...

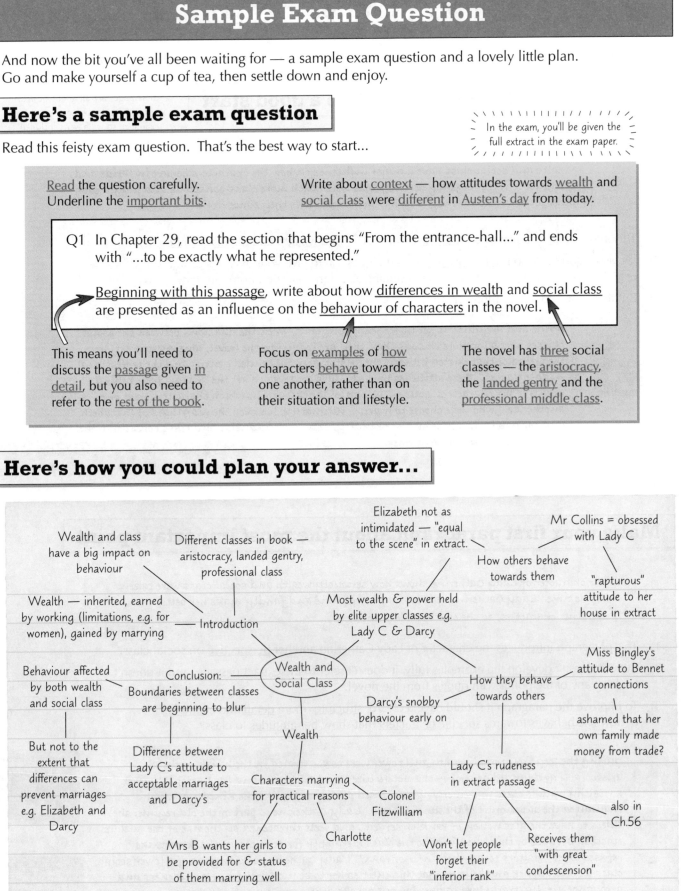

What do examiners eat? Why, egg-sam-wiches of course...

The most important thing to remember is DON'T PANIC. Take a deep breath, read the question, read it again,
write a plan... take another deep breath... and start writing. Leave a few minutes at the end to check your answer too.

Section Six — Exam Advice

Worked Answer

These pages will show you how to take an OK answer and turn it into a really good one that will impress the examiner.

Use your introduction to get off to a good start

These pages are all about how to word your sentences to impress the examiner, so we haven't included everything from the plan on page 67.

You might start with something like...

> Wealth and social class have a major influence on how the characters behave in 'Pride and Prejudice'. In the Regency period, people were much more class-conscious and judged each other on how much money they had and what class they came from.

1) This intro is <u>okay</u>. It mentions <u>attitudes</u> towards <u>class</u> and <u>wealth</u>, and the <u>historical context</u>.

2) It's also a good idea to use the <u>key words</u> in the question to give your essay <u>focus</u> and show the examiner you're on <u>track</u> and that you're thinking about the question from the start.

3) But there's still room for <u>improvement</u>...

This is a clear opening line that links to the question.

> 'Pride and Prejudice' is set in Regency England, when the divisions between the social classes were a lot more obvious than they are today. In the novel, Jane Austen explores the prejudice that existed between the aristocracy, the landed gentry and the professional middle classes. These attitudes towards class and wealth are the driving force behind many of her characters' actions, in particular the way in which characters treat one another and who they choose to marry. Ultimately, however, the marriages of Elizabeth and Mr Darcy, and Jane and Mr Bingley, show that financial and class considerations are relatively unimportant when it comes to love.

This tells the examiner what the essay's about and shows that you've thought about your essay structure.

Make your first paragraph about the most important point

> The character of Lady Catherine shows how seriously wealth and social class were taken at the time. Lady Catherine believes that her fortune and family make her better than the other characters, so she can be rude to them.

1) This paragraph <u>introduces</u> the character of Lady Catherine and her <u>perspective</u> on social class.

2) But... it doesn't <u>develop</u> the examples <u>fully</u>, it doesn't refer to the <u>extract passage</u>, and it doesn't back up any of the points with <u>quotes</u> from the novel.

3) To improve the paragraph it should have a clearer <u>structure</u>, more <u>detail</u> and <u>examples</u> of how she <u>behaves</u> towards <u>specific characters</u> that show her <u>attitudes</u> to class.

> During the Regency period, wealth and power were concentrated in the hands of the aristocracy and landed gentry — characters like Lady Catherine and Mr Darcy. However, a wealthy middle class was emerging, composed of characters like the Bingleys, which challenged the superiority of the upper classes. Lady Catherine is part of the old regime; she "likes to have the distinction of rank preserved", and feels threatened by the rise of the middle classes. Because of this, she clings to the class hierarchy: for example, in the extract, she refuses to let "visitors forget their inferior rank". Lady Catherine sees anyone of a lower social class as beneath her, and believes that this entitles her to be rude to them. Her rudeness and arrogance are illustrated through her language; she dominates every conversation, and offends Elizabeth by telling her that Pemberley would be "polluted" by her middle-class relatives — a very strong choice of word. In this way, Austen satirises the upper classes and shows that wealth and class are no guarantee of good behaviour or manners.

Most exam boards will want you to include some social and historical context.

Analysing the characters' language will help you get top marks.

Referring to satire and Austen's message shows a deep understanding of the novel and will impress the examiner.

Worked Answer

You need to make a variety of points

After you've discussed characters who are <u>strongly influenced</u> by wealth and social class, you might write about a <u>character</u> who has a <u>different</u> attitude towards money and status.

> Elizabeth is less influenced by wealth and social class than other characters. She isn't intimidated or impressed by status and would rather marry for love than money, so she turns down Mr Collins and Mr Darcy.

1) It introduces <u>another character</u> and a <u>different social class</u>.

2) However, you can make this paragraph better by giving more <u>detailed examples</u> and backing up points with <u>quotes</u>.

This makes the link between Darcy's wealthy, upper-class upbringing and his proud behaviour very clear.

> Elizabeth's attitude towards wealth and social class differs from that of characters like Lady Catherine. Although Elizabeth follows social conventions, for example trying to persuade Mr Collins that it would be an "impertinent freedom" to introduce himself to Mr Darcy, she judges people on their merits, not on how rich and powerful they are. This is illustrated when she turns down Darcy's proposal, accusing him of not behaving in a "gentleman-like manner". Elizabeth's criticisms challenge Darcy's belief in the superiority of the upper classes, and make him realise that his privileged upbringing has made him "selfish and overbearing". Austen shows that, in his case, wealth and social status are obstacles that he needs to overcome in order to "please a woman worthy of being pleased" and become a happier, humbler person.

Make sure you use a range of quotes, but don't quote huge chunks. Keep them snappy and relevant.

3) You could also <u>develop</u> it by looking at Elizabeth's <u>background</u> and the <u>effect</u> it's had on her <u>character</u>.

> In contrast to Darcy's upper-class background, Elizabeth occupies a precarious social position, due to her mother's "low connections". Although she has moments of insecurity regarding the "total want of propriety" of her family, the most obvious effect her upbringing has on her behaviour is to sharpen her wits and her confidence in the face of those who judge her. When she meets Lady Catherine, Austen says that Elizabeth "found herself quite equal to the scene", even though others are "awed" or "frightened" by the situation.

Giving original interpretations like this will earn you top marks.

Finish your essay in style

You could say:

> In conclusion, wealth and social class are a big influence on characters' behaviour in the novel. Characters like Lady Catherine show that there was a lot of prejudice against people with less money and power. But some characters like Elizabeth Bennet aren't impressed or intimidated by the aristocracy which suggests attitudes to class were starting to change.

1) This conclusion is okay, but it doesn't summarise <u>how</u> Austen presents <u>different attitudes</u> to wealth and class.

2) So to make it really <u>impressive</u> you could say something like...

> In conclusion, many characters' attitudes and behaviour are influenced by wealth and social class. Lady Catherine represents the attitudes of the older aristocracy; she believes that her money and title make her superior to other characters and give her the right to look down on them. However, Austen uses the characters of Elizabeth and Darcy to show how attitudes towards wealth and status are changing. Darcy initially comes across as proud and snobbish, but his attitude is challenged by Elizabeth, and he overcomes his prejudice. His decision to marry someone "without family, connections or fortune" shows that wealth and status are ultimately less important than love, and illustrates how social boundaries are beginning to blur.

This conclusion summarises how Austen uses different characters to explore the theme of wealth and social class.

Make your last sentence really stand out — it's your last opportunity to impress the examiner.

Why do alligators write good essays? Their quotes are snappy...

It seems like there's a lot to remember on these two pages, but there's not really. To summarise — write a scorching intro and a sizzling conclusion, make a good range of points (one per paragraph) and include plenty of examples. Easy.

Index

The Characters from 'Pride and Prejudice'

Phew! You should be an expert on *Pride and Prejudice* by now. But if you want a bit of light relief and a quick recap of the novel's plot, sit yourself down and read through *Pride and Prejudice — The Cartoon...*

Elizabeth Bennet

Mr Darcy

Mr Bingley

Jane Bennet

Lydia Bennet

Mr Wickham

Mr Collins

Charlotte Lucas

Mr Bennet

Mrs Bennet

Miss Bingley

Lady Catherine de Bourgh

Jane Austen's 'Pride and Prejudice'